The Friendship Solution
Making Friends and Dropping Frenemies

Wayne & Tamara Mitchell

Copyright © 2021 by Wayne & Tamara Mitchell

First published May 2021

Interior and Cover Design: Istvan Szabo

ISBN 978-1-948158-09-1 (hardcover)
ISBN 978-1-948158-10-7 (paperback)
ISBN 978-1-948158-11-4 (epub)

Published by Third Ghost Press

WayneAndTamara.com

This book is part of Wayne & Tamara's series: Asked, Answered, and Explained

"Men's courses will foreshadow certain ends, to which, if persevered in, they must end. But if the courses be departed from, the ends will change."

—Charles Dickens, A Christmas Carol

ACKNOWLEDGEMENT

We want to give special words of thanks to Susan Voskuil and Nadya Yayla. Their constructive critiques and sharing of life experiences sharpened the focus of this book. They gave generously of their time and knowledge.

CONTENTS

Preface 1
Chapter 1: Friends and Frenemies 3
Chapter 2: One Is the Loneliest Number 11
Chapter 3: What Is Friendship? 15
Chapter 4: Peeling the Onion 21
Chapter 5: Come a Little Bit Closer 25
Chapter 6: The Doormat Syndrome 33
Chapter 7: The Answer Is No! 39
Chapter 8: Your Brain Knows 49
Chapter 9: The Ethics of Friendship 53
Chapter 10: Vouching 61
Chapter 11: Honesty 67
Chapter 12: The Friendship Paradox 77
Chapter 13: Ending a Friendship 83
Chapter 14: Moving On 99
Chapter 15: Jealousy 115
Chapter 16: Dangerous Friends 125
Chapter 17: Family as Friends 133
Chapter 18: Romantic Friends 145
Chapter 19: The Power of Friends 165
Chapter 20: Conclusion 171
Notes 177
Works Cited 187

PREFACE

One day, as we were reading an email to our advice column *Direct Answers*, Tamara looked up and said simply, "She doesn't know what a friend is."

That line—she doesn't know what a friend is—has come back to us again and again as we read letters about a problem with a friend. Although we didn't realize it at the time, that is how *The Friendship Solution* began.

We wrote this book for two reasons.

First, when many people use the word "friend," they are actually describing a frenemy, a person they dislike, a rival or an antagonist, or a person who manipulates them. They are not talking about a true friend, someone they know and like, someone they can trust to have their back.

Understanding this distinction is one of the keys to having a good life. But understanding this distinction is not enough. We must act on it.

That is the second purpose of this book. We want to explain why we need to sort people out based on where they should fit in our life.

Some dictionaries define a friend as someone we know well and like, exclusive of sexual or family ties. In this regard, dictionaries are behind the times. More and more, psychologists are seeing our friends, family, and romantic relationships not as fundamentally different but as tributaries of the same river.

That is why when we speak of friends in this book, we include traditional friends as well as relatives and romantic partners.

The Friendship Solution is about the place of friendship in all our relationships. It is about why we have friends, what a good friend is, learning to say no, and letting go of bad friends.

Through letters and research, we will paint a portrait of friendship as it is and as it should be.

Finally, this book is a long answer to a short letter, a letter we got on the day Tamara looked up from an email and said, "She doesn't know what a friend is."

CHAPTER 1
FRIENDS AND FRENEMIES

"The bird a nest, the spider a web, man friendship."
—William Blake, mystic

What would you think if someone asked you to read a murder mystery and there was no murder and no mystery? That's how we feel when a person writes us about a problem with a friend and we can't find a friend in their letter.

Consider these letters from our newspaper column…

Enough Is Enough
I recently agreed to be best man at a friend's wedding, but now I am having reservations and there are only two weeks to go. I sit up nights stressing about this.

Where to start? Four years ago, he came back into my life after a year in which we didn't see each other. At that time he was leaving his wife. I listened and said I was there for him.

I was in a bad situation myself, living on my own, feeling isolated and not going out. Anyway, one night, he went off with a group of three girls leaving me on my own in a bar. I went home and later he turned up at my house with the girls.

My friend started a relationship with one of them, and this is the girl he is marrying. After the girls left that night, he came up to me, patted me on the head as though he were the big man and said, "I love you, Erik." Since agreeing to be his best man, this memory haunts me for some reason.

This friend becomes angry if I speak longer than a few seconds, and he finds a way of interrupting me to divert attention back to himself. Only recently I realized he uses personal information, which is borderline inappropriate to mention, to knock me off my stride in conversation.

For example, in front of other people he said, "You were in a worse situation than me when we met up again, weren't you?" Another time it was, "Your parents must have worried when you were a baby and did projectile vomiting." He is also fond of using the term "bless you" in an extremely patronizing way.

He brings these matters up when I am speaking about something entirely unconnected. Usually his behavior doesn't dawn on me until after the fact, when I leave his company deflated.

Now I avoid him and don't return his calls. I've heard others refer to the sinking feeling you get when someone's caller ID appears on your phone and you don't answer. I get that every time. I've confronted him, but it doesn't change anything.

I am not a perfect person, and I know everyone needs a mirror held up to them. I'm sure my behavior in some way contributes to the situation. I just wish I could find a way to stop this dynamic as it happens, because at the moment all I can do is go back to him and say, "When you said X the other day, it was a problem for me because..."

I feel I would be doing myself a disservice by being his best man but fear backing out will make me look bad and possibly cause me to lose the respect of others in our social circle.

-Erik

Erik, good people always think they have a part in creating sour relationships and bad people never do. This is a telling sign about good people, even as it is their downfall.

We cannot take on guilt for the actions of another. The problem is bad people will allow us to do that again and again. When we don't let conniving people suffer the consequences of their behavior, we deprive them. They won't learn. They won't grow. They won't change.

That's the only thing you should feel guilty about.

This man has gone through life doing what he is doing to you. What better lesson could he learn than having a man he doesn't respect back out of his wedding?

Some people might want you to enter a lion's cage saying, "When you roared, it made me feel..." We would tell you to arm yourself with a whip, a chair, and a pistol.

You don't say you are angry, but you are. Anger is one of our most valuable self-defense mechanisms. Listen to it and act from it.

-Wayne & Tamara

Identity Theft

I've known my best friend for six years. Initially I thought she was a great person who was there for me in times of crisis. As time went by I noticed she was very competitive with others, and then I saw she was most competitive with me.

She will ask what I am wearing then wear something shorter or more low-cut. She sees me in something then buys that exact item. She copies phrases I say and repeats facts from me and claims them as her own. When we were in college, she constantly tried to one-up me in grades and games, even cheating to do so.

I confronted her after a close mutual friend brought this to my attention. I tiptoed around the issue because I did not want to hurt or insult her. She said she competed with everyone but not me, because with me she feels she cannot compete. After that, I let it go.

Not to boast, but I am an attractive person, and her male friends always ask about me. I only mention this because I know she is insecure, even though she is an attractive girl who is physically fit, smart, with many friends.

When I moved, she purposely "forgot" to pass on invitations to a wedding and to a reunion of college friends. She forgot my birthday then tearfully explained it was all a misunderstanding. Mind you I live five minutes from her house, and she did not even pick up the telephone.

You cannot get into a car without her speeding to show you how fast she can go or be in a group without her trying to appear more intelligent than you in conversation. I see the person she is inside, and I don't like that person.

Part of my problem is during college she was there for me financially when my family could not be. I will always love her for that. Even though I paid back every dollar, I still feel indebted. Sometimes I think she only helped me so she could feel superior.

-Hailey

Hailey, who you are is a compilation of all you have experienced. You were raised to be good and polite. You have a sense of style and a sense of self. But your friend is invading your identity.

Robbers in a home invasion might take a homeowner's gun and use it against her. You may not own a gun, but you own a sense of niceness and your friend is using that sense of niceness against you. The word "nice" comes from a Latin word which means to be ignorant. You are not ignorant of what is going on, but you are ignorant of your own best interest.

She is injuring you. When you fail to confront her, you are not being honest, and being honest outweighs being nice.

You've seen inside her, and you don't like what you see. The only way to take back your identity for your sole use is by severing this relationship. Don't be nice. Be honest.

-Wayne & Tamara

And finally…

Friends?
I met my friend when we were in graduate school, and we enjoyed hanging out together outside of classes. After receiving our degrees, we both left school to live in different states. That was 10 years ago.

We've kept in touch, but our phone conversations and twice-a-year visits became opportunities for my friend to talk endlessly about her problems. When I tried to fill her in on my own life, she obviously tuned out.

In the past few years, I've not visited her at all and dread her occasional phone calls and visits to my house. She invites herself now because I no longer invite her. When she's at my home, she literally follows me from room to room, talking nonstop, until I make an excuse to get away from her. I tell her I need to take a nap, but I don't sleep. I sit in my room and read or enjoy the quiet.

Here's the worst part. She and her family, including two young children, are moving to our city. Her family has a small income, and they are buying a house in a grand neighborhood they can't afford. She asked if she and her husband and her children can stay at my home on their trips to our town to deal with house matters.

My husband and I have no children. Even though our home is tiny and perfectly sized for us, I let them stay. She told me her husband would start his new job before they finished purchasing this house. I felt obligated to offer him our guest room. If I hadn't offered, she would have asked anyway.

Now he's here, and it turns out he'll be staying on through the weekends. I am seething.

I would never, ever, under any circumstances impose on a friendship this way. I feel used, resentful, and don't care if I ever see her again. Should I end this friendship? I'm getting absolutely nothing from it but a knot in my stomach.

-Lorraine

Lorraine, life hands us lessons all the time. When we don't learn the lesson, life gets more and more difficult until we do.

You were making and accepting calls from a woman you didn't want to talk to. Now her husband is living in your house. Furthermore, she plans on moving in with her two small children. Where does this lead? Count on being a free, drop-in babysitter. Count on her asking you to pick up her kids after school. Count on imposition after imposition until you finally learn to say no.

Tamara often uses the example of oatmeal cookies. If you don't like oatmeal cookies, don't be "polite" and say you do. Otherwise you will always be offered oatmeal cookies and friends will make you gifts of oatmeal cookies. That is why you cannot fake emotions out of a false sense of politeness.

Everything is being done to the advantage of your "friend." Nothing is to your advantage. This arrangement isn't working, and her husband needs to stay elsewhere. It is too much of an imposition. Call her tonight and tell her. Pick a day soon, like Friday, and tell her that will be his moving day. Let her know she and her family must make other arrangements when they move, whether their house is ready or not.

Don't waste time on long explanations or sugarcoat it. Make the call short and factual.

-Wayne

When Lorraine wrote back to us, she said, "You are so absolutely positively right. I am messaging my husband right now to discuss our visitor's last day. I think what I found most helpful is your pointing out that I'm accepting calls and visits from someone I don't even want to talk to. It's so crystal clear. Thanks for giving me the kick in the butt that I need."

These letters remind us of a line from Thoreau. "To say that a man is your friend means commonly no more than this, that he is not your enemy."

Lorraine thanked us for the kick in the butt. With her husband's help, she was ready to act. But it takes more than a kick in the butt for most of us to act upon a problem.

We once read a book which made a distinction between positive knowledge, negative knowledge, and ignorance. By positive knowledge, the author meant we think we know something and we are right. For example, Paris is a large city in France. Negative knowledge means we think we know something but we are wrong. Paris is a large city in Italy.

Ignorance means we don't know where Paris is and we know that we don't know. Usually people think ignorance is bad, but actually it is a good state to be in. When we know we don't know, we are prepared and willing to accept the right answer.

Negative knowledge is the worst state of all. We are wrong and we don't know we are wrong, so we are unwilling to give up our beliefs.

A friend is someone we like, trust, and respect. A friend is someone we feel a bond with. A friend is a favored companion.

A friend is not necessarily someone we work with or went to school with. A friend is not necessarily a neighbor or someone we rub elbows with at church or at the place where we volunteer. A friend is not necessarily someone we share a history with.

Often those people are frenemies.

What is a frenemy? We use the Oxford University Press definition. A frenemy is "A person with whom one is friendly despite a fundamental dislike or rivalry."[1] That's our working definition.

Knowing who is not a friend, and acting upon that knowledge, will save you a lot of pain and countless misunderstandings.

CHAPTER 2
ONE IS THE LONELIEST NUMBER

"Loneliness is now so widespread it has become, paradoxically, a shared experience."

—Alvin Toffler, futurist

We think of friendship this way.

A mirror is lonely. When we appear in a mirror, we feel that loneliness. But when we see a friend, our loneliness vanishes. It is as if, when we see a friend, we spring into existence.

When the poet John Donne wrote, "no man is an island," he was mistaken. We are all islands and friendship connects us. We crave companionship. As William Hazlitt wrote about a friend, "I know I can get there what I get nowhere else—a welcome, as if one was expected just at the moment."

That's how friends make us feel, as if we are welcome and expected, just at that moment.

When Lord Byron's beloved Newfoundland died, he wrote a poem in honor of the dog. Byron called his dog the first to welcome him and his firmest friend. He even built a monument to the pet. Byron's friend John Hobhouse contributed these words to the epitaph: "Near this spot are deposited the remains of one who possessed . . . all the virtues of man without his vices."

When Tamara was a little girl, she and other children went to a farm of a distant relative. The farmer had a draft horse named Bartleman, and the children climbed a ladder to get on Bartleman's back.

When apples were in season, they rode Bartleman to an orchard and picked apples off a tree from atop the horse.

When Bartleman died, a longtime neighbor of the farmer volunteered to call a rendering plant to haul the carcass away. A rendering plant, if you don't know, collects dead animals and turns them into fats, oils, and fertilizer. What this man suggested was putting a chain around Bartleman and dragging his body into the bed of a large truck to go to a rendering plant.

At the suggestion, the farmer knocked the other man out cold. Bartleman was his friend, and the farmer buried the horse in the field where he died.

We can be friends with animals because we share with them the three basic traits of friendship. They keep us company; they make us feel more relaxed and secure; they make us want the relationship to continue.

A year ago, we ran across a friendship questionnaire designed by researchers at McGill University.[1] The questionnaire measured the degree to which a person fulfills the qualities of a friend, and it listed qualities of friendship such as stimulating companionship, sensitivity to emotional states, and loyalty.

As lifelong dog owners, the first thing that occurred to us was that our dogs would get a higher grade on the questionnaire than many people. Many needs listed on the form could also be met by a cat, a parrot, or Bartleman.

Friendship, even with an animal, gives us the recognition we seek from another conscious self.

In Daniel Defoe's famous tale, Robinson Crusoe finds himself shipwrecked on a deserted island. In despair he cries, "Oh that there had been … but one soul saved out of this ship … that I might but have had one companion … to have conversed with!"

Loneliness is the worst of feelings. It calls up a primal fear and the memory of waking in our crib, believing we are alone in the universe. It drives us to other people, and sometimes it drives us to be "friends" with the wrong people.

One is the Loneliest Number

In the movie *Cast Away,* Tom Hanks is marooned on an island when a package containing a volleyball washes up on the sand. Using his own blood, Hanks paints a face on the ball and names it Wilson.

Alone, Hanks shares his thoughts, hopes, and despair with his silent friend Wilson. Finally, desperate to return to civilization, he builds a raft and leaves the island with the volleyball.

Though Wilson is lashed to the raft, waves and wind loosen the lashes and the volleyball floats free. When Hanks realizes what is happening, he tethers himself to the raft for safety and swims after his friend. But Wilson has drifted out of reach.

In desperation Hanks cries out, "WILSON!" Then, grief-stricken, he cries, "I'm sorry, Wilson. Wilson, I'm sorry! I'm sorry!"

A song says one is the loneliest number, but that doesn't answer the question What is Friendship?

CHAPTER 3
WHAT IS FRIENDSHIP?

*"I wonder whether you ever think of the place
of friendship in life ... what it is..."*
—John Masefield, poet

When Daniel Hruschka, an anthropologist at Arizona State University, wanted to define friendship, he sought a definition that would include not only industrial societies but also nomadic herders, small-scale farmers, and hunter-gatherers. He wanted a definition broad enough to include people from all times, past and present, and from every continent.

There was really only one place for Hruschka to go—Yale University.[1] In 1935, Yale started gathering information about cultures and societies around the world. That collection morphed into a database which today includes thousands of cultures and is usually considered the most complete in the world.

In his book *Friendship*, Hruschka describes how he whittled those thousands of cultures down to the more manageable number of 60.

Hruschka settled on a definition of friendship as "relationships of mutual affection and support."[3] In short, friends help one another in times of need and they feel positive emotions toward one another. That's the core pattern of friendship.

Friends are different from strangers and acquaintances. With strangers and acquaintances we respond in one of two ways; either we act from our sense of politeness and manners or we understand the relationship is tit-for-tat, like a business transaction. You do something for me, and I will do something for you.

But true friends share and help as the occasion arises without counting the immediate cost.

Daniel Hruschka's definition of friendship is abstract, but Lydia Denworth, a science writer, put it more concretely. Speaking about the effects of conversation with a good friend, she said, "I mean it literally affects your blood pressure, your sleep, your stress responses, your immune system, all of those things."[4]

Contrast that with our working definition of a frenemy. "A person with whom one is friendly despite a fundamental dislike or rivalry."

When Juliet Holt-Lunstad, a psychologist, conducted a meta-study of over 300,000 people, she found that friends reduce our chance of early death by half, and the health benefits compare to quitting smoking or starting to exercise.[5]

In a study involving more than three million people, Holt-Lunstad found living alone, loneliness, and social isolation had worse health effects than obesity. And this is true for people of all ages.[6]

Canadian researchers John Helliwell and Haifang Huang put it another way; they found that doubling the number of friends in real life affects our subjective sense of well-being as much as upping our income by 50%.[7]

Think about who a friend is and then apply it to this depiction of a friend and a girlfriend.

The Equal Friend

I have a good friend I've known five years. We met when I lived out of state, prior to the birth of my daughter. She's never met my daughter, but we stayed in touch over the years and frequently exchange email and pictures. She sends my daughter gifts for her birthday, Christmas, and other occasions.

What is Friendship?

Since my daughter was born, I've separated and started dating again. I've been seeing the same woman for a year, and she's very opposed to the gifts my friend sends my daughter. She thinks it's weird, and there's an argument anytime a gift is received.

She doesn't want anything to do with my friend, despite my friend trying to be her friend. My girlfriend says she has a right to be upset and compares it to a situation where I got upset because she accepted a gift from a coworker.

On that occasion, when a coworker told her he liked her as more than a friend, she told me she would stop spending time with him and wouldn't accept any gifts from him. A month later, she accepted a birthday present from him and I was offended she accepted.

I don't think the situations are comparable. My friend, over the course of five years, has never expressed interest in me or made advances. We've just been good friends. I told her that were it more, I would be the first to do something about it.

Does my girlfriend have grounds to be upset? Should I tell my friend not to send gifts for my daughter?

-Tom

Tom, the soldier and poet Henry Howard, beheaded by Henry VIII, once observed that the happy life contains good health, a quiet mind, and "the equal friend." By an equal friend he meant a companion with whom we have no quarrel, no strife, no jealousy, and no hidden intentions.

Howard's phrase "the equal friend" sticks in our minds. When someone is your boss or subordinate, you are in a tricky situation because you are not equals. But you are lucky. The friend who sends your daughter gifts is an equal friend.

We would not say the same of your girlfriend. An honorary "aunt" sending gifts to your daughter is not the same as a girlfriend accepting gifts from a man who wants more than friendship. The situations are not comparable.

You caught your girlfriend with her hand in the cookie jar and chastised her. Now, as payback, she wants to admonish you. The problem is your hand wasn't reaching for a cookie.

Giving in to someone who badgers us seldom solves problems. Though it is the easy course, it creates more prickly situations. There is no reason your friend cannot send gifts to your daughter. There is better reason to question whether you and your girlfriend belong together.

Henry Howard began his list of good things by saying, "My friend, the things that do attain the happy life be these…" He then offered a test. If what he said is true, at day's end you will find "the night discharged of all care."

Compare your friend and your girlfriend and decide which one of them discharges all your cares.

-Wayne & Tamara

Friendships share common traits, though none of our friendships are identical. Different friends bring out different things in us. But typically we share most of the following qualities with authentic friends.

Friends accept us.

Friends encourage us.

Friends give us warmth.

Friends listen to each other.

Friends share good intentions.

Friends share a common identity.

Friends are not possessive or jealous.

Friends accept openness with each other.

Friends are people we want to be with.

Friends accept changes in the relationship.

Friends share secrets without fear of betrayal.

Friends are honest in their expression of emotion.

Friends touch and permit themselves to be touched.

What is Friendship?

Friends share feelings, often without talking about them.
Friendships are mutual, with each feeling the back and forth.
Friends share and sacrifice for each other, without counting the cost.
Above all, friends touch us where we live.
And, as Emerson said, "To have a friend, you must be a friend."

There is another way to think about friendship. But to tell that story we need to mention Robin Dunbar and the years he spent living among gelada monkeys.

CHAPTER 4

PEELING THE ONION

It is not so much our friends' help that helps us, as the confident knowledge they will help us.

—Epicurus, philosopher

Gelada monkeys live in the high mountain meadows of Ethiopia. They gather in large groups, and they are baboon-like, with large, fluffy manes.

Geladas are the only grass-eating monkey. They are not good at climbing trees and they spend as much time on the ground as we do.

In the 1970s, Robin Dunbar lived among these monkeys, a day's ride by horseback from the nearest road.[1] Dunbar noticed that geladas spend as much as a fifth of their day grooming each other. That's much more time than is needed to clean each other's coat. It was obvious the monkeys were using this time to bond, or, as we might say, to make friends.[2]

In the early 1980s, Margaret Thatcher's government reduced funding for scientific research, and Dunbar, an anthropologist, was out of work. He turned to journalism. The switch gave him time to pour over the observations he had laboriously collected.

About the same time, a new idea began circulating among primatologists and anthropologists. The idea was that the size of an animal's neocortex (what Dunbar calls "the thinking part of the brain") might be linked to the size of their social groups.[3]

By now, Robin Dunbar was living among millions of people in London, and he wondered what this idea might mean for human beings. Using a ratio of neocortical volume to total brain size, he calculated that the average number of people in a person's social group should be about 150.[4] Any number larger than that would be too great for the brain to handle.

This number, often called the Dunbar number, is the number of people we call casual friends. One hundred and fifty is actually an average, spanning a range from 100 to 250 for different people. Though we called 150 the Dunbar number, there are actually five more Dunbar numbers.

Imagine human social groups as circles within circles, like layers in an onion.

On the outer layer are about 1500 people, the number of people whose face we can recognize and put a name to. In the next layer are 500 people, our acquaintances, the people we know well enough to hold a conversation with.

Going deeper are our casual friends, the group of 150.

There are three more layers in the onion. The next layer has 50 people, our close friends. That group is followed by a group of about 15. These people, called our sympathy group, are individuals we can confide in about most things. About 60% of our social effort is directed toward this group of 15.[5]

Finally, in our innermost layer is a group of five or so people, our closest friends. Dunbar calls these people our "shoulder to cry on" group. They are our best friends, our true intimates. They offer us the greatest emotional support, and they may include one or two family members.

Keep in mind these group sizes are averages only. Also, women have more friends than men, extroverts have more friends than introverts, and older people have fewer friends in the outer layers, though about the same number in the inner layers.

Robin Dunbar offered this way of thinking about the inner three groups.[6] If we throw a large barbecue party in the summer, the guests will likely come from our group of 50. Hosting a small dinner party, the attendees will come from our group of 15. And if we are seriously stressed, we will turn to our group of five.

Dunbar also observed that humans have spent 95% of their evolutionary history as hunter-gatherers, and hunter-gatherers alive today have an average (mean) group size of 150 (actually 148.4).[7] Moreover, that happens to be the group size of hunter-gatherers in times past.

Dunbar numbers suggest that the number of relationships we can manage depends on two things: our brain capacity and the amount of time we have available.[8] The brain can handle social groups only to a certain size and relationships consume time. It takes time to share a cup of coffee or hold a conversation. Time spent with some people is time we cannot spend with others.

You might wonder in these days of social media, when the term "friend" is fuzzy, if the numbers hold up. Well, some researchers found the number of postings on Facebook and Twitter track roughly with Dunbar group sizes.[9]

More impressively, researchers examined a massive telephone data set of billions of phone calls. When statistical physicists were called in to make sense of the data, the results showed, as Robin Dunbar says, "You can see these layers beautifully laid out."[10]

The ultimate reason behind human social group size is controversial, but we find Dunbar numbers useful for one reason. They provide a way to think about the people in our lives and what position they should occupy.

Since we can manage only so many relationships and our time is limited, we need to surround ourselves with the best friends we can find.

These are the Dunbar categories.
- Can match name to a face
- Acquaintances
- Casual friends
- Close friends
- Confidantes
- Best friends

Don't interpret the word friend too narrowly. Friends may include tennis friends, relatives or family members, coffee shop friends, spouses, friends of friends, live-in partners, coworkers, dates, neighbors, or classmates.

In Chapter 1, we met three people: Erik, who agreed to be best man for a man who patronizes and belittles him, Hailey who calls a competitive woman she doesn't like a best friend, and Lorraine, who has an out-of-town friend she can't stand seeing or talking to.

All three situations are a train wreck. Each involves a frenemy.

If you feel uncomfortable with a friend or best friend, odds are you have them in the wrong mental category. You treat them as though they belong in one category when they clearly belong in another.

You may need to boot some people from close friend to acquaintance. Others may belong in your outermost circle, where their relationship to you is no closer than this—you can match their name to their face.

Dunbar circles are a first tool you can use to figure out where a person belongs in your life. Having a mental idea where they fit will make it easier to deal with them.

In the next chapter, we'll examine another measure of friendship. Closeness.

CHAPTER 5
COME A LITTLE BIT CLOSER

"Friendship is almost always the union of a part of one mind with a part of another. People are friends in spots."
—George Santayana, philosopher

I have been best friends with Alexis for 12 years. We met when we were already out of high school and had our own individual set of friends, but we grew to be the best of friends.

She personifies what friendship is. She is loyal, dependable, and generous with her time, her energy, and her care. What a beautiful person! She has countless friends. Many of them actually compete over her.

She grew up with a friend from high school who moved away six years ago. In the meantime, we became very close, and she remained close to her other friend. Once Alexis started working at her new company, she met new people and grew meaningful friendships with a handful of them as well.

In the past year or so, I have felt our meaningful friendship is no longer all that sacred. I see her carry herself in the exact same way with pretty much all her friends. She's been the maid of honor at several of her friends' weddings, and she seems to be everyone's best friend.

I can't tell what I represent to her anymore. It seems as though anyone in her life could be replaced by another and she would carry on with the same dynamic in every relationship. It deeply hurts!

We've always been there for each other. She and my husband are good friends through me, and she comes over quite often for dinner, drinks, and just to hang out. At a certain point, people even called us the happy trio.

Yet at other moments she still refers to her out-of-towner friend as her best friend. It almost makes me feel like a fool. I've opened up my heart, myself, and my home to this girl, yet she calls someone else her best friend and makes no effort to try to be subtle or refrain from saying it, thinking that maybe it would hurt me.

Ever since then I have been wanting to see her less. I feel unappreciated and betrayed and don't get excited anymore when she wants to come over or hang out. In fact, I'd rather not.

Should I talk to my friend or should I keep my mouth shut at the risk of sounding petty or possessive? Or should I simply distance myself from her without saying anything? I don't want to turn to my other friends fearing this will simply turn into a source of gossip more than anything.

-Olivia

Olivia doesn't know whether to talk to her friend or to distance herself. But that's not the issue. Olivia doesn't understand who Alexis is.

In the 1980s, Sarah Matthews, a sociologist, interviewed the generation who lived through the Great Depression and Second World War.[1] She found these people fell into three different friendship styles.

The first group she called the Independents. These people didn't identify any one person as a friend. One man told Matthews, "I'm my own man… Do I have friends now? I have people that I know." Sarah Matthews found that, despite what we might think, most of these people were neither lonely nor isolated. They simply didn't have close friends.

Matthews called her second group the Discerning. These people collected a small number of close friends over their lifetime. The drawback to this pattern of friendship is that, as one ages and friends die, these people become increasingly alone.

The Discerning were probably the group Samuel Johnson had in mind when he said, "If a man does not make new acquaintances as he advances through life, he will soon find himself left alone. A man, sir, should keep his friendship in constant repair."

Matthews named her final group the Acquisitive, which was a poor choice of names. Synonyms for acquisitive are greedy, grasping, and avaricious and that does not at all describe these people. A better name for them would be Adventurously Outgoing.

These people move through life collecting friends as they go along. They typically have many friends from different periods and places in their life.

The Adventurously Outgoing are like jugglers. The more balls they have in the air the less each ball will get touched. But the juggling is exciting. Just because you won't be touched much doesn't mean you want out. "Keep me in the rotation! Woo-hoo! I got touched and I'm up in the air again."

Olivia doesn't understand that Alexis is one of those people who collect friends throughout life. Rather than being upset that Alexis looks at someone else as her best friend, Olivia might take comfort knowing that, of all the people in Alexis' life, she is in an inner circle.

In the previous chapter, we mentioned people often don't know who their friends are.

My best friend Becky and I have known each other since we were 12. We are now both 48. Nine weeks ago, I broke my ankle and was on the couch for eight weeks. This left me horribly housebound, not even able to get myself a cup of coffee or drive because I needed crutches.

Becky's husband is our financial planner. The week after I broke my ankle, he called my husband to do a financial review. I know he wanted to move our money around since this is how he earns commissions. We hadn't heard from them since Christmas, and the sole reason he called was business.

Even though my husband told him it was a bad time because I had broken my ankle, I did not get a phone call, flowers, or a card from them. I thought perhaps they were having some kind of financial troubles and put it down to that.

Last weekend, I flew to another city for a wedding and stayed with my sister-in-law. I was still in a cast and using a cane. Low and behold, on Sunday my sister-in-law tells me she is having guests over but won't tell me who. My mouth fell open when a car pulled up and it was Becky and her husband.

They were in my sister-in-law's city for a convention. I was gracious and polite while Becky showed me her new two-carat diamond ring and told me they bought a house in another country so they can escape our cold winters.

This morning, I received an email from Becky—again, not a phone call—asking to come over so her hubby could do business. I burst into tears. My husband's reaction was we should pull our business away from her husband and find another financial planner. This would be a slap in the face, and I'm not sure I want to go that far.

My husband also suggested we reply to the email saying we are going to go visit those who helped me convalesce and take them gifts of appreciation. He thought they would get the hint. What would you do?

-Carolyn

Carolyn, when the wife of an attorney we knew would mention they were going to a party, he would sometimes correct her. He would say they were "going on the clock." This attorney understood that much of his business originated from social occasions.

Most of us don't think the people we occasionally call, like our plumber, are friends, but many people think the accountant or planner they socialize with is a friend. And they may be. But they may also be using friendship as the shoehorn they need to make a living.

Though it's unpleasant to consider, your lifelong "friend" and her husband may think you aren't making them enough money to send you a gift. They may believe you have dropped below the level at which they need to be polite.

We wouldn't give Becky credit for the email she sent. Email takes no time and effort. She could do 16 of them in her bathrobe before lunch to help her husband make money.

We start from this premise: it is not wise to make emotional decisions about money. If you think you can do better with a different financial planner, then move your business. But if her husband is making you money, email back, "When we are ready for a financial review, we'll let you know."

If these two knew you might move your account, they may treat you better—the way a new financial planner, anxious to keep your business, would act. But remember, there is never an advantage in letting someone move your assets around just to generate a commission.

Your 36-year friendship appears to be less than what you thought. That's actually a plus. It is always better to know who our friends are.

-Wayne & Tamara

If we added something to our answer, it would be this. Carolyn needs to understand the concept friends of utility.[2] Friends of utility are those who focus on the benefits of the friendship. These relationships are less true friendship than friendship based on advantage.

The next letter is from a young woman who was in a romantic relationship. At least on his side, it was a friendship of utility.

For an Old Friend

I dated someone for five months last year. By the time we'd dated long enough for the "relationship talk" to come up, he had an important audition on the horizon. Questions of commitment were put on hold pending the outcome.

Neither of us imagined he would get the job because, well, it's kind of the holy grail to people in his line of work. Many, many try for it and very, very few succeed.

But he did get it. In the space of a couple of weeks he was yanked out of my life, moved away and on top of the world at his new insanely high-profile, fairy-tale job. He has fan pages now, a huge paycheck, and people coming out of the woodwork by the hundreds to pat him on the back.

We're still "friends." We go to lunch whenever he's in town, but in between we don't talk or email much; he was never much of a phone or email communicator even when we were together.

He never said so much as a "thank you" for anything—the shoulder rubs, the messages wishing him luck, the time spent fielding a billion phone calls from a billion people so he could concentrate on acing his audition.

His lack of response to my efforts hurts. Trying to talk to him like a normal person doesn't help; he'll respond with humor to the details of my conversation but completely ignore anything with the slightest emotional context.

Staying together after he got the job was always mutually understood not to be an option. In short, he was not there for me. This isn't new or surprising; his distant, unsupportive behavior appeared as a potential relationship red flag while we were dating.

We worked together, and I still work here, so I have to listen to people talk about him constantly. My public attitude has never been anything but supportive, but the truth is I'm heartbroken, angry, and unbelievably hurt.

It could all be over for him in a few years, and then again, it may not. Then I'll be seeing his photoshopped face plastered on the side of buses and buildings.

I've got projects for which I'm getting positive feedback, and I'm happy with my life. That he accepts my loyalty and friendship without attempting to return it hurts. I don't know what I can do to feel any resolution.

-Laura

Laura, Edmund Morris, Ronald Reagan's authorized biographer, tells a revealing story about the former president. During one presidential campaign, Reagan headquartered on a Virginia estate.

At dawn of his first day there, people awoke to the sound of an ax. Outside, Ronald Reagan was chopping down a stately tree. Beyond the tree lay fields, woods, and mountains.

Reagan didn't own this property, and he didn't own the tree. He didn't have permission to cut the tree down. Nonetheless, that's what he did. Asked to explain himself, he replied simply, "Because it spoils the view."

Little acts reveal character. While dating, you noticed this man's distant manner, though you loved his star persona. But how much of the real man did you acknowledge?

Though personable on the outside, he is cold and callous. You never had the power to make him a sensitive, thankful human being. Ask yourself why you loved someone who treated you so.

We have one suggestion. If the success of any one of your projects could be advanced by a letter or good word from him, ask. A man like him understands this sort of request. It won't bring you emotionally closer, but it could advance your career.

It was never an issue that you would relocate with him. Like Reagan's tree, you spoiled his view.

-Wayne & Tamara

Research confirms there is often a mismatch between who our friends are and who we think they are. A study by four investigators affiliated with MIT analyzed connections between students in a business management class.[3] These students ranged in age from 23 to 38, and each was asked to rate every member of the class on a scale from "I do not know this person" to "One of my best friends."

Ninety-four percent of the people thought their feelings were reciprocated, but that was true only about half the time. One of the researchers, Alex Pentland, suggested a reason.[4] We fail to read friends correctly because that helps us maintain a favorable self-image.

This study was sensationalized as "Only half of your friends like you!" However, others had a different take on the experiment. Said one, "So while it's true [only] around half of the friendships in the study were mutual, it still found close to three-quarters of your friends like you."[5]

In 1992, Art and Elaine Aron, along with Danny Smollan, published a scale to measure how close we feel toward another person.[6] The scale is called the Inclusion of Other in Self Scale (IOS), and it looks like a first grade arithmetic worksheet.

It is a nothing more than seven pairs of circles, beginning with two circles side by side and ending with two circles which almost completely overlap. In between are circles which progressively intersect.

Using the IOS scale, people are asked to mark the picture which best describes their current relationship to another. (If you find this hard to visualize, cut out two circles and experiment with moving them into each other until they represent your degree of closeness to someone else.)

George Santayana said, "People are friends in spots," and the IOS scale is a way of thinking about those spots. The greater the overlap we share with another, the greater the intimacy and the deeper the friendship.

Carolyn, whose friend bought a second home in another country, and Laura, left behind by a highflying boyfriend, came to understand just how little overlap they shared with their "friend."

Dunbar circles are one way to think about where a person should fit in your life. The IOS scale is another.

As we said, to have a good life, we need to mentally put people in the category where they belong, based on their behavior. Second, we need to act from that understanding.

We realize you cannot always escape from people who are not true friends; they may be permanent fixtures in your work or social circles. But at a minimum, it is helpful to understand where they fit.

Remember Erik in Chapter 1? Let's take a look at his problem from another angle.

CHAPTER 6
THE DOORMAT SYNDROME

Oftenest men in friendship but a faithless haven find.
—Sophocles, playwright

Erik was asked to be best man at the wedding of a man who patted him on the head, interrupted his speech, and revealed inappropriate information about him to third parties. Erik wrote, "I'm sure my behavior in some way contributes to the situation."

We agree, but not in the way Erik thinks. Erik believes the flaw in the relationship is partly his fault. We think he understands the word "friend" far too loosely and is sending out signals he can be taken advantage of.

In the 1980s, two researchers in New York, Betty Grayson and Morris Stein, wanted to learn how criminals size up potential victims.[1] To do this, they surreptitiously filmed people walking down a sidewalk. Then Grayson and Stein showed the film to 53 violent convicts.

The inmates were asked to rate the pedestrians on a 10-point scale ranging from "A very easy rip-off" to "Would avoid it, too big a situation." To help understand the ratings, Grayson and Stein asked professional dancers to analyze the film.

When the dancers did a body movement analysis, they found potential victims were subtly less coordinated than non-victims. That was interesting, but there was still a problem with the research. The film clips didn't show people in a standard setting wearing freely flowing clothes.

Two decades later, Lucy Johnston of the University of Canterbury in New Zealand led a group to reexamine the study.[2] This time, participants wore only black body suits equipped with lights or reflective markers. The film of their movements showed nothing but the way their joints moved, as points of light against a black background.

The results were startling. From the movement of joints alone it was possible to detect mood, gender, and whether someone was likely to be a victim. Johnston then investigated whether a brief self-defense course would help the vulnerable people appear less vulnerable.[3] It did not.

But when the participants were trained how to walk in a different way, their vulnerability ratings plummeted. Retested a month later, their vulnerability ratings were still low.

What does all this have to do with Erik?

Like many people, Erik is sending out signals he is vulnerable to being used. In some people, the signal might be their posture. In others, it might be their good manners or politeness. In still others, it might be their people-pleasing nature.

The lesson is simple. If friends take advantage of you, you need to alter the way you behave with them.

I am hoping you might be able to provide some advice on a professional relationship. I will try to be succinct.

In August, I had the opportunity to change jobs and begin working closely with two people I considered to be my friends. I will call them Marge and Alice. The two knew each other through me, and the three of us were enthusiastic about working closely with one another.

Very soon after we began our new job, it became abundantly clear Alice was not only a terrible teammate but also somewhat unstable. She failed to meet deadlines or respond to emails that didn't come directly from management, missed meetings, passed her work off on other people, and was completely uncommunicative.

On top of that, she did many things that made it obvious she was trying hard to make herself stand out above the rest of the team, even if it meant using others to get what she wanted.

I am confident in my abilities and not afraid to stand up for myself, so even when Alice's actions began to infringe on my ability to do my job, I did not stress. I confronted her and our superiors and righted the situation in a professional manner.

My concern is not for myself. It is for my good friend Marge. Every day I see Marge becoming angrier and angrier with Alice. Her anger and hatred for Alice seem to be consuming her completely. Today was a tipping point when Alice convinced our boss to offload some of her responsibilities, which are already much less than anyone else's, onto Marge.

Marge is completely the opposite of me. She refuses to stand up for herself, always worried that she will offend someone. I can tell she is being destroyed by this relationship, but I also know she loves her job.

Going to our management doesn't seem to be a solution because, I believe, they see Alice through rose-colored glasses.

I want badly to mediate this situation and find peace for Marge, but I am afraid that since Alice has also committed offenses against me, it will be difficult for me to remain neutral. Not only that, but Marge is so afraid of confrontation she will not agree to talk to Alice with me or let me talk to Alice on her behalf.

What do I do? Do I just sit back and watch my friend suffer?

-Carol

Carol, some people say, "No good deed goes unpunished."

It's one thing to go to the boss and say you have a problem with Alice. It's another to mention Marge's problem. It labels you a buttinsky, and it suggests you may be the problem.

The dynamic between you, Marge, and Alice appears to be other than what you thought. The dynamic previous to the formation of the team was ignorant friendship. Now that you are in a team environment, you see them in their true colors. These two are less your friends and more people who create problems for you. It is better to see them more as coworkers and less as friends.

You can't make a person who is passive and non-confrontational into a person who is active and willing to engage. That can only change when Marge feels strongly enough to overcome her fears and fight back. Perhaps she will have her Popeye moment. "That's all I can stands and I can't stands no more." But getting to that point can only be gotten to by her.

You solved your problem with Alice. You found a way to manage her. Marge hasn't asked you to intervene and she does not want you to intervene. Don't jeopardize your solution for Marge's sake.

We can't fight another's battles. Marge won't learn anything if you try, and very possibly your good deed, like many good deeds, will not go unpunished.

-Wayne & Tamara

In her book *The Doormat Syndrome*, psychologist Lynn Namka asks how do you know if you are a doormat?[4] She answers, "You still have mud on your face from the last time you tried to help someone who walked all over you."

Putting it more professionally, Lynn Namka says, "Doormats become hooked into feeling good by pleasing someone else."[5] What she is talking about is not altruism. She is talking about people who repeatedly sacrifice their own needs for the needs of others. Though they may feel they are acting from principle or good manners or kindness, they are really acting from fear.

You can read book after book on psychology without running across the word *courage*. Psychology makes almost nothing of courage, which is a mistake. We can't feel noble about building self-esteem, but we can feel proud of ourselves for displaying courage.

Courage is facing what threatens us—the second time. The first time our response might be automatic and thoughtless. We may not acquit ourselves well. But later encounters with the same problem give us the opportunity to demonstrate courage. We can learn to say, along with a character in Shakespeare, "Boldness be my friend! Arm me, audacity."

But how? We'll say how in the next chapter. For now, the thing to remember is that anyone who uses you as a doormat is not your friend.

Rewiring
Our divorce will be final in five weeks. My wife blames me for everything that went wrong in our relationship, and I admit some things were my fault. However, in the time we were together she never once said she was sorry or understood where I was coming from.

Foolishly I still feel obligated to her. She calls and asks me for favors. She starts talking nicely then tells me what a horrible person I am. I leave these conversations feeling emotionally and spiritually drained. I don't want to say hurtful things to her, yet I need this to stop. I guess part of me still hopes for reconciliation.

-*Ozzie*

Ozzie, your wires are crossed. Abuse and love are opposites. Once you uncross your wires it will change your whole perspective. It will shed light on new relationships as well as your old one. For the next five weeks, to thine old self be true. Once the divorce is final, change your phone number. Your wife has given you a great gift, the chance to discover what love actually is.

-Wayne & Tamara

The cowering dog's cowering brings more abuse. That's the fundamental lesson people suffering from the doormat syndrome need to learn.

In a classic experiment, the psychologist Martin Seligman shocked dogs until they gave up trying to escape the shock.[6] Later, when put in a situation where they could escape, the dogs would not even try. They would lie down and whine.

Seligman called this condition "learned helplessness," but that is a misnomer. The dogs didn't learn to be helpless. They gave up hope, and because they lost hope, they stopped trying.

Giving up hope was the first order effect, and becoming helpless was a second order effect. The condition would be more aptly called learned hopelessness.

If you have a problem standing up for yourself, you may simply be like Seligman's dogs. You aren't helpless. You've given up hope that you can change. But hope, even when buried deep within us, can be reawakened.

One thing flows logically from a discussion of the doormat syndrome. The next chapter.

CHAPTER 7
THE ANSWER IS NO!

Never say the yes
you don't mean, but the no
you always meant, say that,
even if it's too late
even if it kills you.[1]
—Carol Rumens, poet

I'm 19. For almost five years I've been in a close trio with two of my best girlfriends. I'll call them Jen and May. Jen just moved back here to go to college and now lives with me for the summer, so we've been spending a lot more time together.

Recently, May called us and spent an hour complaining about how we constantly leave her out of our plans and how she feels we're pushing her away. The thing is we both realized we are! May has been a toxic friend for a long time.

Every time we hang out, she constantly talks about the drama in her life! If Jen or I try to change the subject, she brings it right back to herself.

May asks for our honest opinions and gets angry at us when we give them to her. She has terrible anger issues and snaps at us for the tiniest of slights. We can't take this friendship anymore, but we can't gradually drift away because she clings to us desperately.

-Cassidy

Cassidy, the sooner we realize we craft the situation around us by what we allow, the sooner we can sculpt the life that we want.

If you pull away from May, she won't think, What I am doing is wrong. She will think what you are doing is wrong. It doesn't matter. Grab your life by the reins and say, "Whoa! I'm not having this."

-Wayne & Tamara

Do we need to say more than this? The sooner we realize we craft the situation around us by what we allow, the sooner we can sculpt the life that we want.

No Honor
I am in an awful fix! My best friend is getting married and wants to make me her maid of honor. Normally, I'd be ecstatic, except for one thing—I can't stand her fiancé. The man she is marrying is emotionally abusive, and there is a distinct possibility he's cheated on her more than once, though I do not have concrete proof of this.

The engagement itself surprised me as she expressed doubts about him, particularly the issue of his fidelity. I spoke to her then about my feelings, and the conversation nearly ended our friendship! To make matters worse, she forced me into agreeing by asking me in public in front of others.

She knows I am not a gossip and would never do anything to make her uncomfortable. I could not decline graciously or even put off an answer. I've spent more time getting to know her fiancé, hoping to see what she sees in him, but each time I've come away more disgusted with this man and more convinced she is making the most horrible decision of her life.

-Genevieve

Genevieve, your best friend is forcing you to be a hypocrite. If you stand up for her at her wedding, you are saying, "I accept that these two should be man and wife and spend their lives together." No, you don't accept that. You don't believe that at all.

If you accept, she will see you as a willing participant in her choice and come to you as an avenue of consolation. Only by declining her offer can you prevent playing the hypocrite for the length of her marriage.

-Wayne & Tamara

A friend doesn't force you into this position. The bride-to-be used emotional blackmail to get what she wanted. No one who does that to you is a friend, and if you let someone force you once, it will happen again. And again.

Three-Ring Circus

My friend has a crazy personality when she drinks. As I've grown closer to her over the past year I've seen that alcohol transforms her into a completely different person. I've always known she thinks my fiancé is good-looking, but this did not bother me until last night when I went with him to her birthday party.

She got extremely intoxicated and started asking my fiancé for hugs. As she hugged him she slurred that she would like to have his baby. Then she would go off in a completely different direction and say she is like a mother to me, and if he ever hurt me, she would hurt him.

Later, she said if anything happened to us, he knows who he could come to for comfort. That was just the beginning of her comments. I felt awkward. Her friends didn't know what to do. They looked at me wide-eyed wondering what I would do. I laughed it off as if it was funny, but I was offended.

Something similar happened a few weeks ago, and now that she has done this a second time, I feel she is compromising our friendship. The worst part is she is supposed to be in my wedding in three months. I am deeply concerned she's going to embarrass me at my wedding.

Part of me wants to drop her as a friend because I would never in a million years do this to her. Part of me wants to rationalize this away, say she was just drinking, and talk with her about it. She may have no clue what she was doing because she called today to thank me for the present I gave and acted like everything was fine.

-Rosemarie

Rosemarie, circuses are fun, but not when the tightrope walker falls from the wire, the tigers escape from the cage, and elephants rampage through the crowd. This woman will turn your wedding into a circus. She has a problem with alcohol and discussing it with her will only lead to angry denials.

Your wedding can be a treasured memory or fodder for TV shows specializing in mortifying wedding videos. Drop her from the wedding party, and if you are serving alcohol at the reception, withdraw that invitation as well. Don't let a drunken woman become the ringmaster of your special day.

-Wayne & Tamara

Although Rosemarie may think this woman's behavior is getting worse, we suspect Rosemarie is simply seeing the woman for who she is.

Some people are clueless about the power of names, which is why they are so poor at naming things. Shy people, who want to learn to stand up for themselves, often look to the field called assertiveness training. But the name itself is a problem for them.

The word assertive is too close to aggressive, and aggressiveness means pushy, overbearing, and belligerent. For shy people, this is what they are afraid of.

If you struggle accepting the word assertive, think of it as we do. The word simply means standing up for yourself, which is our right.

When we hear someone say, "I do not like confrontation," it is almost as if they are saying, "I don't know how to tie my shoelaces." But learning to tie shoelaces is a simple skill, and so is learning to stand up for yourself. Both take practice and both have a straightforward solution.

The first step in learning to stand up for yourself is identifying the emotional barriers which make you inclined to avoid confrontation. Damon Zahariades, in his excellent book *The Art of Saying No*, lists some of the reasons people are afraid to say, "No."[2]

They are people pleasers.

They feel saying no is rude.

They feel upset when they say no.

They don't want anyone to say no to them.

They are afraid of disappointing others.

They want to take the easy way out.

They want to help others.

They want to be liked.

If any of these apply to you, you may have a fundamental misunderstanding about saying no. Saying no, when it is appropriate, causes people to respect you; saying yes when you shouldn't causes people to disrespect you.

As Zahariades says, "Once you possess the ability to say no with confidence and grace, and do so with regularity, you'll notice changes in how others perceive you."[3]

There's another lesson here as well. Some of your so-called friends want you as a friend not because they are your friend but because they think you are a pushover or because they want to use you. These "friends" you need to drop.

Saying no is not an ability people are born with. It's a learned skill, and if you are a people pleaser, you've handicapped yourself. Saying no is neither mean nor selfish. And helping others to your own detriment is not a virtue.

Standing up for yourself is no more than frank communication. Another word for frank is honest. It is such a paradox: you fear the response from others if you say no, when their response will be to respect you more.

A man, who struggled to say no all his life, told us he realized the power of no when he was standing in a post office line. A woman rushed in behind him, explained that she was late for class, and asked to jump ahead of him. In that moment he had a realization.

He had every right to his place of line, and he also was in a hurry. He said, "No," and in that moment had the unfamiliar sense that it felt good. The sky didn't fall, the building didn't collapse, and fissures didn't open in the earth. All he said was no, for good reason, and he felt the power of gaining control over his life.

Perhaps Genevieve, who is being coerced into being a maid of honor, or Rosemarie, who may allow a drunken woman to ruin her wedding, are too weak to stand up for themselves now. But with practice their bad habit can disappear.

The key is to start small, as with a clerk who tries to upsell you, and say no. Start small and build until saying no with grace and tact becomes a habit. It's like escape velocity in rockets. The hard part is getting the rocket off the ground, but then it takes much less energy to keep the rocket moving.

Self-Defense

I am one of a group of mothers with children in the same preschool. We share play dates together. At one play date with two other mothers at my house, one of them became angry with me.

I couldn't think of a thing I did to offend her, so I asked the other mother. She couldn't think of anything either. She suggested confronting the first mother, but I decided against that, thinking if she was truly a friend she would approach me.

But she didn't. She stayed angry. I think she is jealous of the rapport the second woman and I share because our children are the same age. The first woman has gone to extraordinary lengths to make me feel excluded when we are all together. She invites the other woman to events without extending the invitation to me and my daughter.

I am finding it harder and harder to be in the group without her taking a passive stab at me. I no longer want to be friends with her, but that also means I have to give up my other friends and so does my daughter, which is not fair.

Every time I try to turn down invitations from women in the group, they won't let me bow out gracefully. If you haven't guessed by now, I do not like confrontation. How can I back away without hurting feelings and making it more awkward?

-Pat

Pat, most of the lasting lessons we learn are from our parents, and often those lessons were never directly taught. If you are passive, your daughter may learn to always give in to people who act badly. Solve this problem for yourself and you are likely to solve it for her as well.

Reacting appropriately in each situation, instead of reacting the same way in all situations, is a valuable skill to possess. Though being passive works sometimes, if your only defense is avoidance you will often find yourself defenseless, as in this case....

-Wayne & Tamara

Pat needs to realize she has every right to be in the group. This woman will succeed in punishing Pat if Pat lets her.

A man writes...

I have been friends with a female for eight years. At first everything was good as we share the same hobbies and lifestyle choices. Over the years I've noticed she is selfish and competitive, especially with my girlfriend. She is the type who will see an article of clothing on a friend then run out and buy the same thing.

Once she overheard a friend talking then bought the car her friend wanted and proclaimed she had always wanted one. Common courtesy is less important than her need to stay on a par with her friends' fashion. I find this extremely irritating. If you have bad style it may be a problem, but the fix isn't to copy everything your friends do.

Which leads to my present problem. Recently she bought a portable music player and now wants me to dump my entire music library into it. Is it easy to do? Yes. But it has taken me 10 years to compile my music collection, researching music from movies and magazines, buying CDs, downloading songs, and spending days organizing the software.

She has the nerve to ask for it as if it is no big deal. She does little to work for things but somehow gets what she wants because she has no scruples about asking. Am I the selfish one?

-David

David, people say imitation is the sincerest form of flattery, but that isn't correct. Imitation is the sincerest form of identity theft. Your music is your soul. Like a diary, it is the story of your life, and like a diary, it is not for publication. Tell her that, and then tell her you know she will understand.

People often put nice ahead of no. To their own detriment. No means no. It doesn't call for discussion, debate, or reasoning from the other party. If you let her engage you in a discussion, you will be on the defensive and you will forget what is best for you. Your answer is your answer.

-Wayne & Tamara

We knew a woman, going through a divorce, who was awarded the house in the settlement. The last time she saw her mother-in-law, that woman asked if she would give her the house. A house!

Some people will ask for everything until you learn to say no.

The Right Direction

One of my best friends asked me to be his girlfriend. I like him as a friend but nothing more. How can I tell him no in a way that won't make us stop being friends? Please answer as quickly as possible.

-Marci

Marci, when you learn to say no, your life gets a whole lot simpler and a whole lot happier. Saying no is often difficult, but it's much easier than saying yes to something you don't want.

Tell your friend that you just want to be friends. Don't offer an excuse, an explanation, or leave any doubt that your answer is no. Often it is not possible to give a reason, like trying to explain why you like blue and not yellow.

You don't have to justify your feelings to anyone else, and offering lengthy explanations makes things worse. He can't argue with a simple, polite "No." Attempts to save his feelings now will result in more hurt feelings later and give him hope where there should be none.

You can't find happiness in life without moving in the direction of your true feelings.

-Wayne & Tamara

Another woman has the same issue…

I need advice on building personal boundaries. Simply put, I have a guy friend who has feelings for me I don't share. We dated briefly, I broke it off, and we continued as friends.

While we are both acutely aware I'm not interested in an intimate relationship with him, he's made it clear I am the object of his affection. He does not respect my personal space.

We argue a lot, especially if he ends up crashing at my house after a night at the pub. Even when I tell him he can only sleep on the couch if he comes over, he weasels his way into my bed. I feel I am enabling him because I don't want to hurt his feelings and usually say yes when he asks for a favor.

I am a passive person. How do I identify and develop my core beliefs, values, and boundaries?

-Sue

Sue, when you break up with a man, it's not wise to go to "Let's be friends." That's like teasing a dog with a treat you are not going to give him.

You don't need to identify core values as much as you need to act from what you know. You say you don't want to hurt his feelings when you should be saying, "I don't want to hurt my own feelings."

You have been given a gift of intuition, but you keep trying to give the gift back. Your intuition is more powerful than your reasoning and more powerful than your false sense of good manners. It's time to begin to follow it.

Learning to act from your feelings is like going to a fitness center. Slowly you will grow stronger; slowly you will grow bolder; slowly others will respect you more.

Start with little things. Practice being true to your feelings again and again. When someone expresses an opinion you don't share, without apology tell them your beliefs.

But don't practice with this man. He's in your past. He is about to learn, as Anne Lamott says, no is a complete sentence.

-Wayne & Tamara

This chapter has been about standing up to people who want you to act against your own interests and beliefs.

When you doubt yourself, it might help to remember that your brain knows who your friends are.

CHAPTER 8

YOUR BRAIN KNOWS

To like and dislike the same things, that is indeed true friendship.

—Sallust, Roman historian

Alexander Nehamas tells a story about his friend Tom.[1] Once, when Tom was a houseguest, Nehamas needed to take his child to school. It was a rainy November day and on impulse Tom decided to come along. He quickly tossed a raincoat over his pajamas.

When Nehamas arrived at the school, he realized he had a flat tire; a philosopher at Princeton University, he hadn't the slightest idea how to change a flat. But Tom, in pajamas, raincoat, and bare feet, leapt out of the car and changed the tire in full sight of the arriving parents and children.

In his book *On Friendship*, Nehamas tries to explain why he and Tom are friends. Tom is practical while he is not. Perhaps opposites attract. Then again, he and Tom share common interests. Perhaps like attracts like.

But no matter how much Nehamas thinks about their friendship, he cannot explain why he and Tom are friends.

Carolyn Parkinson, a neuroscientist at UCLA, might have the answer.

When Parkinson was at Dartmouth College, she, Thalia Wheatley, and Adam Kleinbaum scanned the brains of pairs of friends in real time as they watched videos.[2]

In one video, an astronaut shows what happens if you wring out a washcloth in space; in another, journalists debate the use of humor by Barrack Obama; in a third, a man explains why he nominated himself as Australian of the Year. In all there were 14 videos, ranging from cringe comedy to a baby sloth sanctuary to highlights from a soccer match.

What Parkinson and her colleagues found was that friends see the world the same way. To put it more technically, friends share neural activity, as measured by functional magnetic resonance imaging (fMRI) of their brains. Friends of friends also share in neural activity, but they share a little less. Friends of friends of friends share less still. After that, the effect dies out.

If you are thinking birds of a feather flock together, so were we.

In an earlier chapter we mentioned the IOS scale as a way to measure closeness. Brain scans are another way, though few of us will ever have access to brain scans.

What is fascinating is that from fMRI scans it is possible to predict if two people are friends. It is also possible to gauge the social distance between two people using brain scans. And in an earlier study, Parkinson and her colleagues learned that as soon as we see someone, our brain tells us where they fit into our social network.[3]

We can think of a social network as our web of ties to the people in our life. Social scientists represent these ties by considering each of us a node, or point, with lines drawn to every other node (person) we connect with.

When they do this for every person in our network, the result is a tangle of lines that show how our entire social network is connected.

Partly by choice and partly by chance, we live in a social network. Our choice of friends shapes much of our network, and our network shapes us. That's why it is so important to have the right people in our life. Frenemies make our life difficult. Friends ease our path.

Take these two letters for illustration...

Wheelman

My best friend told me she was going to hang out with her boss's son. She asked me to cover for her with her boyfriend. If her boyfriend called, I was to say she was with me but in the shower or something like that. I didn't have a problem because I'd covered for her in the past.

The next day, on the freeway, she said she had something to tell me. She had sex a few times with her boss's son the night before. When I asked if this was a one-time thing, she said it wasn't and she was going to see him again. Now I feel torn by the knowledge I have to keep from her boyfriend.

-Cindy

Cindy, you're an oven mitt in your friend's kitchen. She thinks your function is to keep her from getting burned.

You cannot let another destroy your character. Don't let her make you a liar, a hypocrite, and an accomplice in her behavior. In an armed robbery the driver of the getaway car is just as culpable as the one who held the weapon.

-Wayne

Full Circle

Six years ago, I started dating Philip, a man nine years my senior. We dated for three months and he kept our relationship a secret from everyone. Later, I dated one of his friends, and we fell in love and married.

It was not until I dated my husband that I learned while I dated Philip he was living with one woman and dating another. Yes, three women at one time. But since I was happy, in love, and married to the man of my dreams, it was of no consequence.

Three years later, Philip has no job and no place to live. My husband says he can live with us until he gets on his feet. He lives with us a year and a half, free of charge, with no job until the last two months. When we asked him to pay a modest rent, he agreed.

He makes the first payment then moves out—and in with my mother! My mother has a history of bad relationships. Her typical man moves in, takes everything she has, and moves on. Needless to say, I am floored. Philip contributes next to nothing to her financially. He's cheated on my mother twice that I know of.

On Monday, my mom tells me they are getting married. I tried talking to her and I tried begging, but she thinks he is perfect. I know she is about to make the biggest mistake of her life, but she thinks I am trying to hurt her. We are not even allowed to know when or where the wedding will occur.

-Brenda

Brenda, your mother's lack of good judgment shaped your life. She raised you as a woman who would consider dating a man in secret, and she made you a woman who would share her home with a scoundrel and mooch.

When you kept Philip in your circle of friends and sphere of influence, you in effect vouched for him as a good person and trustworthy man. Now this cad is about to be your stepfather. That's regrettable, but it's poetic justice for your mother.

The lesson here is that bad things not squelched in the beginning come back to haunt us. You saved a snake from the cold, and when he warmed up, he bit both you and your mother.

-Tamara

Our friends reflect our character, which is the focus of the next chapter.

CHAPTER 9
THE ETHICS OF FRIENDSHIP

Show me your friends, and I will tell you who you are.
—Greek proverb

Aristotle divided friends into three categories: friends of utility, friends of enjoyment, and friends of virtue.[1]

Friends of utility are people who use us because it is to their advantage. Think of study partners who cozy up to us because we know the subject matter better than they do. They may have nothing to contribute, but they know we do.

Friends of enjoyment might include friends from a softball league or a bridge club. Wayne knew a boy who became a well-known political cartoonist. He had many friends of enjoyment because he was a natural comedian, and people considered him a friend because he was so amusing.

The last of Aristotle's categories is friends of virtue. Friends of virtue are people whose character we respect. When Aristotle created this category, he was suggesting there is an ethical ideal for friendship.

This goes back to a point we made previously. Our choice of friends shapes our social network and our social network shapes us.

My friend Helen asked to borrow money or the bank would take her house. The money Helen borrowed I was saving for new carpet in my house. When I asked for it back, she said she lent the money to her friend Sandi, who is having an affair on her husband. Helen promised to repay the loan once Sandi repays her.

Helen is also having an affair, and I even covered for her with her husband by saying she was with me. In August, I charged the carpet on a no-interest, no-payment credit card. If I don't get the money back by February, I owe the whole amount plus six months of finance charges.

If I take Helen to court, all of this including her cheating will come out in the wash. What can I do to save this friendship and get my money back?

-Karen

Karen, we make our own future but in a way so subtle most of us can't figure it out. Involving yourself with deceitful people in a web of deceit was bound to come back to haunt you. If you lie down with dogs, you get up with fleas.

Perhaps a lawyer could help. But if you can't get your money returned, consider it the most valuable lesson you have learned in a long, long time.

-Wayne & Tamara

Pants on Fire

I have a "friend" with a problem. This girl has a problem with lying. She lies to her friends, family, everybody. It's not just little white lies. It's huge, boldface lies.

Starting when she was a teenager, she's been telling boyfriends she is pregnant. Her mother has even gotten calls from her exes asking how their "child" is doing. Of course, these children do not exist.

Her latest story is over the top. She told this guy she was carrying his child and went so far as to post someone else's old ultrasound pictures online. When confronted, she either denies she did it or claims she is still carrying the baby.

Most people won't challenge her because she will do anything and everything to cause trouble for those who tell her she is full of it. I cannot tolerate her anymore. She is so full of herself. Nothing she says is believable.

The Ethics of Friendship

She had a good husband and two beautiful boys and still acts like she is Mom of the Year. Yet she doesn't spend any time with her boys and hops from man to man.

Should someone confront her or should we continue to let her lie? She doesn't realize she is hurting everyone around her. Her mother cut her out of her life and her siblings only deal with her on holidays. What should I do? Probably just stay out of it. Right?

-Elena

Elena, unlike the famous Baron von Munchhausen, who told stories about riding a cannonball and pulling himself out of a swamp by his own hair, your friend's tales are almost believable.

What's not believable is thinking you can make her come to her senses based on your grasp of reality. Dealing with her is like dealing with a walrus, a giraffe, or a crocodile. They simply live in a different world.

People like your friend make the best criminals. They will absolutely never confess. They want to catch you up to their reality. Stick around them long enough and they will make you think you are the crazy one.

Her pathological lying probably started as a way to get attention, sympathy, admiration, or power. Guys like to have sex with her, and she likes it too because she can work her magic on them. Though tales of phantom children may hurt some of these men, it's almost a fair exchange. They get what they want and so does she.

Her history of unstable relationships and estrangement from her family is not in your power to change. Though you would like to protect others from her, they have to experience it and figure it out for themselves.

As you may know, the problem with confronting a pathological liar is, when challenged, they can fly into a rage or become vindictive. Her family has given up on her. You should do the same.

-Wayne & Tamara

People often refuse to see the pattern of a friendship...

I don't drive and have health problems. I have a friend who runs an under-the-table errand service. She is one of my closest friends so I rely on her. I always give her sufficient money for her time, and she has helped me out in many situations.

There have been two times in a row where she has blown me off. Both times she was to take me to a doctor appointment. The first time she did not call me in advance as she always did, so I called her. She said, "I can't talk, I'm running out the door." She hung up before I got to say a word. She called me back at midnight and said she was really sorry, she forgot.

I thought she probably did and went on with my business, though she ruined my plans and I ended up in a jam because of it. Last week, I had another important doctor's appointment. I called her well in advance, and she confirmed it twice during the week. But the time came when she was supposed to call and pick me up, and she never called.

So I called her. There was no answer. Today, she basically blamed the whole thing on me, saying, "I was home sitting around waiting for your call. I don't understand why you didn't get through."

The long and the short of it is I don't know if I am being naïve or if this is just two strange coincidences. I don't want to accuse her of anything, but assessing the situation, I wonder if she doesn't want to do it and won't tell me directly. That would not offend me. I would make other arrangements. What do you think?

-Zeta

Zeta, some years ago, two basketball teams from the state of Ohio were contending for the national championship. The fans from Ohio State thought their team was better than the University of Cincinnati, and they were shocked when the other school won the national basketball title.

For a year, the Ohio State fans claimed it was a fluke that Cincinnati won. But guess what; the next year, the University of Cincinnati won again. That inspired some Cincinnati fans to rent a billboard near the Ohio State campus. The message on the billboard read, "Well, what do you know? Two flukes in a row!"

Why would you expect upfront behavior from someone working under the table? It's time to make other arrangements. Two flukes in a row are a message.

-Wayne

Two flukes in a row are also a pattern. When we see negative patterns, we need to act to end them. Our integrity depends on it.

Over a four-year period I've become great friends with a guy in my small community. He moved into town from a large metro area, and we met through common interests—motorcycling, surfing, and boating. We also share the same sense of humor, same interest in world events, and common interests in just about everything else.

He and I, along with our wives, have become close. I knew all along he'd made a considerable amount of money in the cash advance or payday loan business. I know this type of business has a sleazy factor to it, but I never knew how payday loans actually worked. We were friends, so I wasn't judgmental about his business ethics or morality.

Well, a television network ran a story about these businesses a few weeks ago. They explained how they prey on the poor, the uneducated, and the desperate. People are trapped in super high interest rates, and they can never get out from under them. The business is basically legalized loansharking.

It was an eye-opener. It goes against everything I consider good and right. I was so disturbed by the story I abruptly ended our contact and friendship. This was one of the toughest decisions I ever made, and I've thought about it nonstop ever since. My question to you is have I been unfair?

I don't think you can separate what you do for a living from personal relationships, especially when what you are doing is unethical and immoral, even if it's considered legal. It is true the older you get the harder it is to make true friends, and it sure is tough to give up a good one, but I feel I have to stand up for what I believe.

-Butch

Butch, many people have noted that ancient peoples were just as intelligent as we are. Their beliefs and customs may seem strange to us, but there has been no change in basic human intelligence in the last few thousand years.

What people seldom note is that there are just as many slaveholders among us today as there were in times past. True, slavery is illegal, but if it were legal, some people today would enslave others. Not all those people are in far-off places. Some of them may be sharing your pew in church or riding to work with you on the bus.

In Joseph O'Connor's novel *Star of the Sea*, a character observes that an unrestrained free market "may regulate everything: including who should live and who should die." The economic marketplace, in and of itself, contains no sense of good and bad, right or wrong. That sense must come from within us.

If this man's sense of ethics offends you, feel free to exclude him from your life. Each action we take and each choice we make expresses who we are.

-Wayne & Tamara

Confucius said, "Have no friends not equal to yourself." Most of us would like to be optimistic and philanthropic and think we will drag bad friends up to our level, but it is more likely they will drag us down to theirs.

A contemporary saying has it that if you are the smartest person in the room, you are in the wrong room. In other words, only the people who inspire you, who are in some ways more advanced than you are, can raise you up. That's a terrific way to look at friendship.

Good friends are a positive influence. They help lead us to what we aspire to be. Bad friends are not trying to raise themselves up. They are perfectly content as they are.

A few years ago, the *New York Times* published an article written by a psychiatrist in which he explained how he began pushing a drug for a pharmaceutical company.[2] What fascinated us was the man's apparent naivete.

He wrote, "a friendly representative … made me an offer I found hard to refuse … it would be pretty easy … he quickly floated some numbers … I would be pampered … paid an additional honorarium."

This psychiatrist and his wife were flown to New York where they walked through the "luxurious lobby" of a midtown Manhattan hotel and were greeted with "a dazzling smile." Then they were wined and dined and given tickets to a Broadway musical.

The drug company's techniques were straight out of Dale Carnegie's 1936 book *How to Win Friends and Influence People*.[3] The formula in the book is simple:

Smile.

Begin in a friendly way.

Arouse in the other person an eager want.

Talk in terms of the other person's interests.

Make the other person feel important—and do it sincerely.

Et cetera, et cetera.

What surprised us was that the author of the *Times* article was a.) a psychiatrist, and b.) a psychiatrist visited by drug reps every week. Yet he played Little Bo-Beep about the recruitment process.

He finally quit promoting the drug (after increasing his income by over 20%) when his peers questioned the medication's value.

This was a straight-up friend-of-utility situation. In a similar way, it helps to remember the celebrities we see promoting products on TV are not our friends.

There is another ethical aspect to friendship. It's called vouching.

CHAPTER 10
VOUCHING

I don't need a friend who changes when I change or nods when I nod. My shadow will do that better. I need a friend who will speak the truth and help me with his judgment.
—Plutarch, philosopher

I'm 35 and have friends of all ages ranging from 19 to 70 plus. One of my male friends, 20, has less than stellar morals. For example, he slept with an engaged and later married woman, cheated on past girlfriends, sleeps with an ex he calls "crazy" and "annoying" behind her back, and omits important details about his sex life to his friend-with-benefits girlfriend.

It gets to me, even though I behaved less than stellar when I was 20. I then spent years weeding out people like him from my life because, well, they were toxic, and I spent just as much time working on improving my self-esteem and making better choices.

When he told me about these things, I couldn't help but be repulsed, and I said so. I don't believe in lying or sugarcoating to my friends. Now he's mad and calls me judgmental, when I just feel I have standards.

It was quite an argument. I don't know whether to make amends or walk away because he's so young and it will likely take him time to figure all this stuff out on his own. He also has self-esteem issues.

Am I being too hard on him? If so, is it worth apologizing and saving the friendship? I appreciate your thoughts.

-Lori

Lori, on the surface the idea that we can't judge others sounds plausible, but if you think about it for a minute, and try to apply it, the idea reveals itself as foolish.

If we can't judge others, then there are no role models and no best friends. If we can't judge others, parents can't correct children and teachers can't tell a student when they got it wrong. A moment's reflection reveals that life is nothing but judgment, and if you can't make good judgments, we don't want to share the highway with you.

Those who say you can't judge others are people in the wrong. They say it to disarm people in the right. Good people living good lives don't have a problem being judged, and, in fact, your "friend" wants you to judge him. He hopes you will see him in a positive light as a shrewd chick magnet and man of the world.

If you apologize, it would tell him he was right and you were wrong; his judgment is good while your judgment is bad. A woman may tend to think, I was too harsh. That may be in your nature, but it says something about you and nothing about him.

The most extreme case we've seen of someone unable to make judgments was a woman who, with her husband, owned a cattle ranch. Their mailbox was on a gravel road a third of a mile from their house and barns. Each day her husband would get the mail and keep it away from her because she couldn't cope with the plethora of offers and decisions the mail brought.

At a nursery, this woman could spend two hours trying to decide whether to buy tulips or daisies. Though her husband often worked cattle on horseback, he never took her with him because she wasn't decisive enough to handle a horse.

What does decisive mean anyway? It is a positive way of saying you are judgmental, and being decisive is a positive trait. It means you know right from wrong, up from down, forward from backward.

At some point, holding too much information makes you culpable. If you know this man betrays others and you stay silent, it puts you on the side of the betrayer.

The danger in life is not in making judgments but in making wrong judgments. If this young man doesn't meet stiff opposition, he will grow worse not better. By your own description he is a toxic person, the kind of person you should weed out of your life.

-Wayne & Tamara

If we added something to our answer, it would be this. The world is made worse by not standing up to bad behavior. When people don't stand against bad behavior, say cheating, it becomes a low risk/high reward activity. Bad behavior should always be high risk/low reward.

Digby Anderson is an Anglican priest and a contributor to right-of-center publications. He believes modern society has diluted the meaning of friendship. We don't necessarily agree with that, but in his book *Losing Friends*, Anderson makes one valid point. True friends, he says, should supply us with a network of trust. As he wrote, "It's called vouching."[1]

If Lori, in the letter above, introduces this 20-year-old to friends he might prey on, she has failed in one responsibility. She has, in effect, vouched for someone who lacks character. She is telling her friends he is a good person when he is not.

That's the problem in the following letter.

Company We Keep
I have a male friend I've known several years. He's a player. Always has been and I fear he always will be. I gave his number to a friend, Gloria, who was interested in him. I warned her he's a player; she said she didn't mind.

A month later, I learned another close friend, Cindy, was involved with him, but it was nothing serious. He expressed interest in both of them and said they both knew he didn't want anything serious. One did not know about the other. Then Gloria found a boyfriend and stopped seeing him.

Cindy continued to see him, and it got serious, although he never admitted it. In the past few months Gloria contacted him and he decided he wanted to be with her, but he told Cindy he wasn't seeing anyone else. I felt something was going on but wasn't sure until I confronted him.

I was stuck in the middle. I told him I would tell both women. He didn't tell them, so I did. He got mad at me because now neither wanted anything to do with him. He told me he didn't want to be friends with me anymore.

My two friends were grateful, or so I thought, for letting them know what was going on. Now one friend has decided I should have told her sooner. She says I betrayed her. She will have nothing to do with me. It's difficult as we have the same group of friends. Am I in the wrong?

-Summer

Summer, let's take a broader approach to your question. Do you think a woman should be used as a plaything by a man?

What is a player? A man who plays with women's affections. What are the elements of play in this game? There are two: being involved with multiple women, while concealing that fact, and giving each the illusion there could be more for them, in order to get more for himself.

Both you and this man know a player uses a woman's nature against her. The player says he's not offering anything, but once he is intimate with a woman, she feels it must be a relationship.

You're around a man you know uses women. We are known by the company we keep. You kept company with a man who uses women. Whether you wanted to or not, you vouched for him with your friends. You helped others believe he was all right because he was your friend.

It's as if you introduced a burglar to your girlfriends and he burglarized their houses. Where's the surprise? You knew his nature. Apologize.

-Wayne & Tamara

Vouching

Vouching involves more than honesty. It involves being able to do the hard thing when it is required.

My friend confessed to me that the husband of one of our friends is coming on to her. He sends her emails from a new account and tells her how lovely she is. He also tells her, "I like and miss you."

I went out with my friend and this couple once, and my friend paid the bill. She got a letter from this man criticizing his wife and me for not offering to pay, but he never went out with us before and doesn't know we take turns paying.

My friend also sent him a DVD, which his wife misplaced. He flipped out and was angry at his wife. He said he was so much looking forward to watching the show and his wife does not value her thoughtfulness.

My friend says she is not interested in him. My idea was to tell him that flat out, but instead I told her she is too nice to stop conversing with him. Now he hates me because I won't drive my friend to their house, and, if we have no choice but to go, I insist on leaving early.

What do I do? I can tell him he's a complete jerk, or I can tell his wife, or I can stay silent. If I stay silent I will never speak to him again. I feel my trust has been violated as well, not because he likes my friend but because we are his wife's friends and she considers us family.

-Gwyn

Gwyn, women typically want to be polite and don't want to make waves. They hope a problem will work itself out as some kind of misunderstanding. But the first time your boss slaps your ass or the first time your friend's husband hits on you, you have to say no. When you don't say a clear no the first time, he'll think you've said yes.

This man criticized you and his wife for not offering to pay, and he criticized his wife for not being thoughtful. He did this to ingratiate himself with your friend.

Someone who takes your side when you didn't ask for or need help engages in what is called forced teaming. People who engage in forced teaming invite themselves into your life for the sole purpose of furthering their own aims.

This man put you and your friend in an awkward position.

He is punishing your friend by being the object of unwelcome attention. He is punishing you for knowing. He is punishing his wife for not knowing. Whatever happens, remember there is only one party with blame. Him. What he's done can't be walked back. You can only compound the problem if you don't tell his wife.

Your friend could artfully sidestep the situation by forwarding an email to his wife with a note, "I think your husband accidently sent me an email that was intended for you." Or she could tell him, "One more text like this and I will tell your wife."

But more likely it will fall to you to deliver the news.

If neither of you tell his wife, it makes you both an accomplice to his actions. You are not his friend; you are his wife's friend. You need to stand up for your friend, even if you lose her friendship because of what her husband has done.

-Wayne & Tamara

Vouching is important, whether it protects a friend's sexuality or their bank account.

If we can't vouch for someone, there is no reason to keep them close. At most they should be a casual friend, someone in our group of 150, someone in our social network we cannot avoid.

Vouching is a crucial feature in friendship. It means we give our personal guarantee. It is closely related to honesty, the subject of the next chapter.

CHAPTER 11
HONESTY

"Every time I paint a portrait I lose a friend."
—John Singer Sargent, painter

What is honesty? Some meanings are:
- Free from guile
- Without pretension
- Marked by the truth
- Free from dissimulation
- Worthy of being depended on
- Not disposed to defraud or deceive

Honesty drops the barriers between friends. The further two people are from openness the further they are away from intimacy.

We are often surprised by how frequently people call someone their best friend when there is so much they cannot say to each other. The best friendships are genuine.

My best friend, Ryan, told me last night he got his girlfriend, Rebecca, pregnant. He is 22 and she is 20. He told me he was probably going to marry her "because that is what I should do." Let me give you a little background.

Ryan knew this girl back in high school and met up with her again four months ago. She had just gotten out of a year-long relationship a week before.

Despite that fact, they promptly started sleeping together. Within a month they had a pregnancy scare because she refused to use any form of birth control. She said it "messed with her system."

And he believed her! I told him she was full of it and he needed to at least wear a condom because having a baby at this time in his life would be a disaster. Well, he didn't listen. When he informed me I was going to become an "aunt," I asked him if birth control was involved. He said it got pointless to use any.

I asked if he was in love with her. He said the "in love" part would come along later. Argh!!! I love and care for my best friend, but I have never in my life met such a clueless and gullible guy! He always dates women who manipulate and use him! I am so disappointed.

She does not have a job, skips out on her cosmetology classes, expects her parents to pay for everything she wants, and, to top it off, she is very cold. You know how when you're around someone and you can literally feel they are heartless? Well, that's Rebecca.

She's in his life regardless because of the baby, but he doesn't have to marry her to be a good father. I told him if he was not in love he had no business marrying because it would be mocking the entire institution.

The few times I've been around her, she literally pushes Ryan away when he tries to be affectionate and puts him down in front of everyone. I've been with my boyfriend for three years, and even though he drives me nuts sometimes, I would never put him down due to one thing. We love each other. There is no love between this couple.

It's my belief she has done the classic move of trapping him. Ryan has never felt very manly. He's the baby in his family, and now he has a chance to prove to the world he is grown up! This girl saw all that and fed off those facts. He got trapped; he knew it was going to happen and he let it happen. His stupidity is beyond me!

Ryan appreciates that I am not a beat-around-the-bush person. If I have something to say, I'll say it, though I make it diplomatic and tactful. Should I *go along with this and keep my mouth shut? Or should I tell him what I think and hope he doesn't make the biggest mistake of his life?*

-Liz

Liz, in Stephen King's novel *From a Buick 8*, a character says, "We never go forward believing we are going to fail, do we? No. We do it because we think we are going to save the day, and six times out of ten we step on the business end of a rake hidden in the high grass, and up comes the handle, and whammo, right between the eyes."

You want to know if you should say anything. Of course you should. To do otherwise would put a lie in the middle of your relationship. Tell him not with the expectation he will change, because that's unlikely, but so he understands where you are coming from. You care about him and don't want to see him hurt.

If your friendship can't survive honesty, it shouldn't survive.

-Wayne & Tamara

Another young woman writes…

My boyfriend has been cheated on by every girlfriend before me, so he finds it hard to trust me. But he is trying. His friends manipulate him by claiming I am using him and cheating.

My boyfriend pays for everything for his friends. That's why they don't want me in his life. With me by his side, I don't let it happen. How do I deal with this?

-Amber

Amber, people want to believe the sensational. They want to believe the worst, even with evidence to the contrary.

When his friends told him every girl cheated on him, your boyfriend believed it. You believed it too. But if you haven't cheated, shouldn't that make you wonder if the others were also innocent? You've discovered the motive for his friends' accusations: money.

The difficulty is no one can prove a negative. Once his friends sullied their names and yours, there was no way to undo the damage.

There is one thing you can do. Say to yourself, "I may lose him anyway, so I might as well unleash a scorched earth policy on his friends." Explain to your boyfriend how he is being used. Tell him you haven't cheated, and that's reason to doubt that the other women did.

Leave that idea in his head to fester and fester. He can't unhear what you tell him, and sometime in the future, like a dud bomb from a forgotten war, it may explode. You may well lose your boyfriend, but ultimately this might allow him to be free of his manipulative "friends."

Sometimes all we can do is our good deed for the day and leave things better than when we found them.

-Wayne & Tamara

My closest friend is a dog lover with two big dogs. Although I don't like to do it, I have doggy-sat during a couple of her week-long vacations.

I am an animal lover but like my house clean and odor free. The last time I doggy-sat I covered my floors with blankets and towels. Still the dogs are not well-trained and had three accidents in one week. I had to get my carpets cleaned.

I did not share this information with my friend. Her friendship is important to me and she considers her dogs her family. So I said sweet things about the dogs when she returned and will never say a bad word about them even though my home was left a mess.

I planned to hire a pet sitter for my recent vacation when my friend sweetly volunteered to feed my hamster. She drove over twice during the week to feed the hamster and clean its cage. I expressed my appreciation and gave her a thank you gift.

Honesty

My friend just told me about a trip she is planning soon and I feel terrible not volunteering to doggy-sit. I will feel worse if she asks me to take care of the dogs because I plan to say no. How can I politely decline if asked?

-Keeley

Keeley, openness makes the strongest friendships, and honesty is the easiest way to live. You should have told your friend the dogs had accidents. Once you concealed what happened, it became impossible to tell the truth without making her defensive or disbelieving.

But it's not too late to put things right. Put this on yourself. You are a hamster person, not a dog person. It's simply a difference between you and your friend. Tell her, "I gave it a try and I'm glad the dogs are okay, but I don't want to tempt fate again. Having dogs is too stressful for me."

Suggest kennels or pet-sitting services, or go with her to check out facilities, especially ones with a vet on call. It's what Tamara always says about oatmeal cookies. If you don't like oatmeal cookies, tell people. Otherwise you have condemned yourself to a life of being offered oatmeal cookies.

-Wayne

The following two letters are stark illustrations of Walter Scott's famous lines, "Oh, what a tangled web we weave, / When first we practice to deceive!"

A friend of mine and I began having sex a few months ago. This was pretty stupid because he was involved in a serious committed relationship. I socialized with him and his girlfriend many times, and I don't think she suspected a thing.

He told me all the usual lines. When it became clear they were not true, I stopped sleeping with him.

Last night, I walked into a buzz saw. I went to their apartment. As soon as I walked in the door, his girlfriend screamed at me. I don't know how she found out. I feel angry and betrayed. I want to apologize to her, but I also feel he owes me an apology. He tricked me, and I can't believe that is right.

-Allison

Allison, you want him to apologize for what? For being willing to put one over on you while you were putting one over on his girlfriend?

You knew what you were doing. He knew what he was doing. But you were left out in the cold. That is what you are mad about. Had you acted with character this would never have happened.

-Tamara

Two years ago, I lied (or embellished or fudged, depending on the way you look at it) about my sex life to my best friend. She would not confide in someone if she felt they hadn't experienced what she had.

Knowing that I could, I lied, and I did it convincingly for two years. I mean we aren't talking a lie that ever hurt anyone. Four months ago, I began dating a wonderful guy. I told him the truth about my sexual experience. I would have been okay, but last month I went out of town leaving my best friend and my boyfriend together.

One night they started talking. Thinking she was helping, my girlfriend decided to help him "understand" me. She confided the lies I told her. He was furious because he never heard any of this before. For good reason. It's not true!

Days later, I drove home, and my friend greeted me with all smiles. Then my boyfriend walked in. He glared at me and said, "Who are you lying to?" Just like that I was in a hell I've never experienced. For four hours I pleaded with my boyfriend to believe me while my girlfriend made sarcastic comments.

I guess I lied too well because he decided I couldn't have been lying to her.

In the end, my boyfriend said he couldn't trust me and walked out. He sent a note saying how sorry he was it ended this way. I am devastated. I don't know if I can get him back. Should I try? And what do I do about my friend who basically aligned with my boyfriend to attack me?

-Celeste

The subject line in Celeste's email was the most insightful thing she said. It read: "Trust is a very tangible thing." She's right. We might be able to glue the pieces of a broken vase together, but, like trust, it will never be the same.

When we tell the truth, we have an integrity others can respect, even when they don't share our outlook.

Celeste's letter reminds us of a line from the movie *The Silence of the Lambs*. At one point Hannibal Lecter says, "I do wish we could chat longer, but I'm having an old friend for dinner." Celeste's best friend and her boyfriend "had her for dinner."

When there is a falling out between friends, often the person in the weaker position tries to bolster their stance by taking revenge.

I've fallen out with someone I regarded as a close friend of 10 years. My friend and an ex-boyfriend had an hour-long telephone call discussing my personal life.

I couldn't believe someone I trusted would do such a thing. We didn't speak for months. Eventually she said she was sorry, though our friendship cooled a bit. A few weeks later, she rings and falsely accuses me of stealing another girl's boyfriend. Again, I forgave her.

The next month I had surgery on my knee. Two days later, she sent me a text message asking me to go out. I told her I was on crutches and couldn't go, but she was more than welcome to visit for the evening. I got a text message calling me selfish and saying it was true what my ex said about me.

I tried to call her, but she wouldn't answer the phone. I sent a message back saying if she wasn't going to speak to me, then stop sending nasty messages.

Now she's sent a letter asking if I've been sending her text messages from someone else's phone. Like I've got nothing better to do! I haven't answered her, but part of me desperately misses our friendship. Most of my single friends have paired off or moved away, and I'm finding it incredibly hard to make new friends to trust.

-Elisa

Elisa, your friend sounds more like a tormentor. If you reestablish contact with her, in 10 weeks your life will seem even more chaotic than it does now.

What if you used those 10 weeks to change patterns in your life?

Then, 10 weeks from now, you will not only have learned something, you may have a new best friend, perhaps a woman wise about human affairs. Small decisions about who we spend time with make huge differences in our quality of life.

-Wayne & Tamara

There is a legend about friendship that is 2300 years old. It is the story of Damon and Pythias.

According to the fable, Damon and Pythias traveled to the city of Syracuse when it was ruled by the merciless tyrant, Dionysius. When Dionysius falsely accused Pythias of treason, he was sentenced to death.

Pythias begged for time to settle his affairs and say a final goodbye to his family, but Dionysius refused. Then Damon stepped forward and offered himself as a hostage. If Pythias failed to return, Damon said, the tyrant could execute him in his place.

Dionysius agreed. Pythias left for home, and as fate would have it, his return was delayed by pirates and bad weather. When the day of execution arrived, Pythias was nowhere to be seen, and Damon was scheduled to be slain.

But at the last moment, Pythias sprinted to the place of execution, begged forgiveness for his tardiness, and presented himself to be killed.

According to the story, Dionysius was so moved by the loyalty of the friends that he pardoned Pythias, released both men, and asked to be their friend.

Damon and Pythias are held up as an example of perfect friendship, but the story doesn't make sense to us. Why would Pythias risk his innocent friend? Why would Dionysius spare Pythias? Why wouldn't the bloodthirsty ruler consider killing them both?

We find only one way to make sense of this story. It is symbolic.

Damon is not a real person. Instead, he represents what we might call the character or soul or bond of Pythias. As a person of good character, Pythias made a pledge. He gave his word. When he returned, he made good on his word, and his reward was freedom. Not physical freedom but psychological freedom.

To us, the story is about the reward of honesty. That reward is freedom of mind.

When we stand on our character, the sole reward we should expect is the knowledge we stood on our character. We have remained a friend to ourselves.

That's why Pythias was freed.

The next writer has a huge problem with honesty.

One of my male friends has been cheating on his girlfriend (also a friend) for the past year and a half. They are now looking to buy a house together, but he is still cheating and willing to cheat until he gets caught! I can't tell her as I don't want to hurt her, and I have the feeling she would forgive him anyway and blame the other person.

Problem is the other person is me! I just wish a year and a half ago I never told him I didn't want a relationship, because now I do. We see each other whenever we can, though it's more of a sexual thing. As time goes on I've fallen for him and love meeting him, even if it's just for sex.

-Kylie

We told Kylie, "Our wish is that you surround yourself with people like yourself. If you change, that will be your reward. If you don't, it will be your punishment."

Let us offer one final letter, a letter that seemingly is about honesty.

For months I have known the husband of a friend is battling cancer. Whenever I call and ask in general how they're doing, I hear, "Everything is fine."

I respect that. But it's almost a year now, and I feel like saying, "It's okay, I know what he has been going through. You don't have to tell me anything. I just want you to know you are in my thoughts and I wish you well."

I can't stand the pretense. Should I say what I want to say or continue pretending?

-Mimi

Mimi, people grieve in different ways, people love in different ways, and people have a right to be ill in their own way.

Her husband's medical information is confidential, just like how much they owe on their mortgage or how often they have sex. They have the right not to be reminded of his cancer, and they have a right not to hear trite expressions like, "You are in my thoughts."

There is a difference between caring about others and caring about ourselves. The true measure of compassion is putting another's wishes ahead of your own. Your right to offer threadbare condolences does not trump their right to privacy.

-Wayne & Tamara

Up to this point, we have discussed real friends, people we know in the flesh. But what about online friends?

CHAPTER 12
THE FRIENDSHIP PARADOX

"Proximity is nine-tenths of friendship."
—John Malcolm Brinnin, biographer

"Bonding" is the rather inelegant word psychologists use to express our affection for one another. The term reminds us of chemistry class and covalent, ionic, and hydrogen bonds. We'd rather use words like fondness, affection, or love.

Yet in a way the term fits. We feel connected to others with different levels of intensity.

When we are near a friend, we can express our affection even without words. We lean into each other, nod our head in agreement, or talk with our hands. When we are genuinely happy, we flash a Duchenne smile.

The Duchenne smile is our genuine smile.[1] A regular smile lifts the corners of the lips, but the Duchenne smile lifts the lips and moves the muscle around the eyes. It makes the corners of our eyes crinkle in crow's feet, and it is a smile most of us can't fake.[2]

But how deeply can we bond with others online?

On a Sunday afternoon in 1998 we visited a friend, an engineer, in the American Midwest. After lunch, our friend turned on his computer and began a video chat with two girls living on an island off the coast of Chile.

We have never forgotten the power of that moment. It's old hat now, but it was our first experience video chatting with someone thousands of miles away, in real time and beyond text. It shrank the globe.

In a cynical moment, the computer scientist Robert Wilensky said, "We've all heard that a million monkeys banging on a million typewriters will eventually reproduce the entire works of Shakespeare. Now, thanks to the internet, we know this is not true."

Wilensky was thinking about the amount of claptrap on the internet, and there is no question the internet is home to griefers and trolls, catfishers and doxers. Just like the real world. But on the internet, unlike a book, we are free not to be judged by our cover.

We can share in someone's life and find at least one person to ask, "How was your day?" We can join a community. If we follow a small streamer, they are likely to give us a shout whenever we appear. Moreover, we can sometimes find opportunities to meet our internet friends in person.

Since 2013, most Americans meet their next date online, without friends or their mom knowing who they are talking to.[3]

As in the real world, we will not feel rapport with most people. We all went to school with hundreds of people, yet we probably call only a few of them friend.

Some people believe social media is more helpful for maintaining friendships than for making new friends. Robin Dunbar says, "Seeing the white of their eyes from time to time seems to be crucial to the way we maintain friendships,"[4] and one experiment seems to confirm that.

Pairs of young women, who were friends, were tracked by researchers.[5] They found these friends felt emotionally connected no matter how they linked to each other, but the greatest bonding occurred "during in-person interaction, followed by video chat, audio chat, and IM [instant messaging] in that order."

We believe, however, that the omnipresence of the online world is altering how we connect. To say it another way, evolution isn't done with us yet.[6]

Reaching out to faraway friends is a natural, human thing to do. In Lesotho, the African country with the highest average elevation, paleo-archeologist Brad Steward found strings of beads made from ostrich eggs.[7]

That was intriguing for two reasons. The beads could not have been made there, and they were 33,000 years old. Using strontium isotope analysis, Stewart and his associates determined the beads came from locations from 325 to 1000 kilometers away.

People long ago realized the power of friends in distant places. Perhaps they reached out to guarantee survival in times of scarcity, but we suspect it was for other reasons as well. As Brad Stewart said, "Ostrich eggshell beads and the jewelry made from them basically acted like Stone Age versions of Facebook and Twitter 'likes.'"[8]

But with all the positives of social media there are several downsides.

A link between social media use and depression and loneliness had been speculated about for years. Then, in 2018, University of Pennsylvania psychologist Melissa Hunt found a convincing way to link time spent on social platforms with well-being.[9]

Hunt's experiment followed 143 participants as they used Facebook, Instagram, and Snapchat. With her collaborators, she gathered social media data from each subject's iPhone and had them complete a survey measuring mood and well-being.

Next the participants shared a week's worth of baseline data from their phone. Afterwards, half the subjects were told to use social media normally, while the other half limited social media use to 10 minutes per day per platform.

For the following three weeks, the researchers did a weekly tally on each individual. Then they measured the extent of FOMO (fear of missing out), anxiety, depression, and loneliness in each person. Melissa Hunt reported that, "Using less social media than you normally would leads to significant decreases in both depression and loneliness."[10]

She said this was especially true for people who were more depressed at the beginning of the study. As Hunt stated, "It is ironic that reducing your use of social media actually makes you feel less lonely."

Two years later, when medical researcher Brian Primack ran a related study, he also found a link between extensive social media use and depression.[11] Both Hunt and Primack suggest the culprit is the amount of negative social comparison inherent in social media platforms.

If they are correct, it explains the Friendship Paradox.

The Friendship Paradox is a discovery made by Scott Feld in 1991.[12] Feld, a mathematical sociologist, was interested in social networks. When he compared the average number of friends a person has with the average number their friends have, he found something astonishing.

It turns out that, on average, your friends have more friends than you do.

This is because most of us have few friends, relatively speaking, and a few people have oodles of friends. Think of Olivia who was distressed that her best friend Alexis didn't consider Olivia her best friend. Alexis, remember, was one of those acquisitive people who attract friends from all areas and periods of life.

At the other extreme would be the woman one writer told us about. "From the very first day, she pushed herself into my life like a barnacle attaching itself to a rock."

The math of social networks is complex, but it appears true that your online friends are likely to have more friends than you do. There is even more bad news. Not only do your online friends have more friends than you, they are probably richer than you are too.[13]

So if you come away from social media with a vague sense of discontent, this may be why: other people seem cooler than you are.

One night, we went with a friend to dinner. He drove. We went to a restaurant far from our home and much farther from his apartment near the campus where he was pursuing an advanced degree.

On the way home, on a lonely, dark road, his face shrouded in darkness, he told us the darkest secret of his marriage. Without the shadows, we doubt he would have had the courage to speak.

That is one of the true silver linings of the internet. Its anonymity allows people to reveal their darkest secret, worst fear, or greatest failure—and find a sympathetic ear and possibly help.

Some relationships are a burden. Sometimes friendships must end. Whether we are on the giving or the receiving end, it can be agonizing. But a closer inspection reveals that ending friendships is a normal process.

CHAPTER 13

ENDING A FRIENDSHIP

"I sometimes felt I was the perfect customer for a much-needed but never produced Hallmark card that would read, 'We've been friends for a long time,' followed on the inside by, 'What do you say we stop?'"[1]

—Joseph Epstein, writer

For several years my best friend was Suzie, a woman I knew online. I was in my teens, and Suzie was about ten years older, married with two children. I looked up to her as a mother and sister figure, which was important to me because I don't get along with my real mother and sister.

Suzie told everyone I was her best friend, and I did likewise. I loved this woman beyond measure, and she helped me through some bad times in my adolescence. She said she loved and cared for me too, and I had no reason to believe otherwise.

I went to visit Suzie at her home the summer I was 18. I was supposed to stay all summer, but she abruptly sent me home after a week. The excuse, which I later decided was a lie, was she had a sick relative she had to care for. But we parted with hugs, "I love you's," and "You are my best friend."

Two days after I got home, Suzie emailed telling me never to speak to her again. That's all her email said—no explanation, just "Never contact me again." At the same time she blocked me from all of her websites and removed all entries from her blog that mentioned me. She basically wrote me out of history.

I still have no idea why. We hadn't fought, and I can't think of anything I might have done to offend her, and, believe me, I racked my brains. I was hurt, confused, and later angry. I thought I deserved an explanation, but no explanation was forthcoming. Eventually I moved on with my life, though when I thought about Suzie, I felt puzzled and sad.

A year later, she emailed. She didn't specifically mention what happened but said she'd had mental health issues and marriage problems. She said she'd gotten psychiatric treatment and a divorce, was fine now, and wanted to be friends again. She apologized and wanted my forgiveness.

I wasn't enthusiastic, but I wrote saying I still cared about her and would like to try a friendship again.

Suzie replied with a short note saying she was happy to hear it and would write tomorrow. She never did. I know she was still updating her websites, so it's not like she got run over by a bus. I was more confused than ever.

Two years after that, yesterday, Suzie sent me a request asking to become my online friend! I absolutely adored this woman. I am sympathetic to her as I suffer from depression and know how debilitating mental illness can be. But Suzie obviously has serious issues, and she hurt me very, very badly. Does she deserve a third chance, or do I tell her to leave me alone? I can't decide.

-Caitlin

Caitlin, Joseph Campbell said, "The world is perfect. It's a mess. It has always been a mess. We are not going to change it. Our job is to straighten out our own lives." The question is not does Suzie deserve another chance but, rather, can you have a good life with people like Suzie in it?

You have some pleasant memories of her and a natural desire to help others. But there is always a risk to the lifeguard. A person has to be very strong not to be pulled under by those who are floundering in life. Suzie disturbs your emotional equilibrium and occupies an undeserved part of your mental landscape. Her inconstancy disrupts your well-being.

Ending a Friendship

An old saying claims the essentials for happiness in life are something to do, something to love, and something to hope for. That is a wonderful definition of mental health. Focus on bringing those three into your life. Once you have them, you will feel nothing is lacking, and you will be able to cope with people like Suzie.

-Wayne & Tamara

Some friendships are a burden for another reason…

I have been friends with someone for five years. I always felt she was more attached to me than I was to her, but it never bothered me much. She is a sweet person, and we got along great.

Twenty months ago, her fiancé died suddenly. It was devastating for her and difficult for me. I was friends with both of them. For a long time, I was at her beck and call. If she needed to talk, come over or whatever, I was there for her.

Then, about a year ago, two separate times, I overheard someone ask her if we were sisters. She said we were. I also heard someone ask her if we were roommates. Again, she said we were. Each time I set the record straight.

I took this as a sign she was feeling too close to me and decided to distance myself from her. I hoped once the year anniversary of his death passed, she would find some closure and wouldn't need to lean on me for support.

As you may have guessed, that has not been the case. By being there for her so much, I feel I discouraged her from standing on her own two feet. Now her clingy ways are to the point where I resent her.

At first, I tried giving friendly hints when she called or emailed too much. I said things like, "Gee, I didn't know we had an appointment." But she ignored my hints. If I write anything remotely negative in my blog, she'll check in saying she's worried about me.

A month ago, at a party hosted by mutual friends, she followed me around all night. It doesn't help that I don't feel I can discuss this with others because they all know about her ordeal and will think I am being insensitive. As it is, I feel guilty every time I think or feel negatively about her.

While I like her as a person and still want to be friends, this has been frustrating and stressful. Is there a way to resolve this situation without breaking a heart that's already been broken?

-Greta

Greta, in one episode of the TV series *Midsomer Murders* detective Tom Barnaby says, "Too much grieving will disturb the dead."

There can be too much of wreaths, flowers, and memorial stones. Grieving can kill the griever. Grief needs to find the right place in your friend's life and in yours. You lost a friend when he died. Being wrapped up in her grief is not letting you move on either.

We know a woman whose fiancé stepped into traffic and died 20 years ago. She celebrates the anniversary of his death each year, and she expects special consideration from those around her each time.

We cannot wallow in death. Grief needs to run its course and be put away. It is not a scab to be picked at. We want to live with hope. We want to take off the black. A party is a symbol of life, and at a party you were haunted by the specter of a person who is dead.

A classic pop song says you have to be cruel to be kind. That's actually a line from Shakespeare. "I must be cruel, only to be kind: thus bad begins and worse remains behind." A slow fade from your friend's life would be a kindness to you both.

-Wayne & Tamara

Most of us don't see how ending friendships fits into the context of life. But ending friendships is a natural process, and some societies in the past had formal ways to defriend a friend. With every important event in our lives, who matters most to us changes. As some drop from our lives, others enter.

Each major event in our life alters our social network. Those events include switching jobs, moving, getting married or living with someone, the birth of a child (especially the first child), a serious illness, and death.

When Gerald Mollenhorst, a Dutch sociologist, analyzed social networks, he found something remarkable.[2] In a span of only seven years, about half of close friendships were no longer intact.

Mollenhorst looked at survey results from 1007 people in The Netherlands aged 18 to 65. To gauge closeness, he looked at responses to two questions asked seven years apart. The questions were, "Who do you talk with about important personal issues?" and, "Who helps you with odd jobs [do-it-yourself projects] around the home?"

What Mollenhorst found was that after a gap of seven years, only 30% of people answered the two questions the same way. Although 18% of those mentioned in the first survey were still close, their role in the social network had changed. That meant only about half of close friendships were still intact.

The obvious lesson from this study is, if you are looking to end a friendship, it helps to remember that switching friends is simply what happens in the ordinary course of life.

Spring Cleaning

I met my friend when we were 14, and we instantly bonded. She was funny and fun and exuded the type of confidence that made me enjoy being around her. Through the years we spent great times together, went through many boyfriend changes, and built great memories.

In the last 10 years some of her traits turned to what I consider faults, but I always told myself, Hey, we've all got faults so just let them slide. More and more, however, these traits started getting under my skin—the underhanded comments to make others feel inadequate, the unprovoked competitiveness, the one-upmanship.

I would even go as far as saying meanness.

She will soon be a mother of three and her single friends are not allowed to feel tired or busy. She will go as far as implying that working full-time and raising a family is far more demanding and important than any deadline or circumstance in the lives of single friends, other married people, or married people with only one child.

Her husband is rude and offensive and strikes the meanest comment in public at whoever is his target for the day. To prevent scenes or, worse, making ourselves look bad by striking back, our friends and I just let it slide. We leave with a feeling of complete frustration.

Eventually I decided to spend less time with her, which proved to make things a lot better. Even though I don't talk to her daily anymore, and only see her once or twice a month for the last year, that bad vibe is present every time I talk to her, even when the conversation is short and pleasant.

It leaves me with a feeling of bitterness, which I cannot shake. Somehow, cutting her out of my life seems like too easy an option. I would much rather deal with the issue than simply eliminate the person or our friendship.

What's most difficult is that her comments are so subtle and underhanded. If I do bring up the issue, her response is she was joking or I'm too sensitive. Therefore there is no way to deal with the issue.

I guess my question is how do I remain friends with her without succumbing to the bad energy she leaves me with whenever I encounter her, however briefly?

-Charlotte

Charlotte, you are your own worst enemy. We don't know if you are trying to be the best "good person" on the planet or if you are abusing yourself because you think you need to be abused, but you have almost solved the problem. However, something internal prevents you from seeing it.

Severely reducing contact with this woman has helped you feel far better. Still, you want to hang in there as the friend who can make her dif-

Ending a Friendship

ferent. Not only do you lack the ability to change her (you have tried and failed), you don't have the right to make her someone she isn't. In the same vein, she has no right to a friend she mistreats.

She can't be approached about her behavior and her husband is as bad or worse than she is. There is no point in rewarding them with a friendship which is not repaid.

The Gestalt psychologist Sheldon Litt said, "Many conflicts can never be solved, but they can be abandoned, and therein lies the solution." You want a better life? Leave this nasty couple alone. It's wasted time, wasted energy, and a waste of your life. You are not improving her life. She is pulling your life down.

Turn the problem upside down. Ask yourself, "What am I avoiding by wasting my time and energy on this woman?" If you back off from this two-person calamity, you can be an inspiration to the rest of your friends. That's the best way to help yourself and to help them.

One key to a good life is to keep only things and people which enhance it, while eradicating everything else.

-Wayne & Tamara

There is a saying that a stranger is just a friend we haven't met yet. The saying is absurd. When we meet someone new, we have no idea if they will or should be our friend. It takes time for people to reveal their true colors. Only then do we know if they can be our friend.

Trust is built slowly, a little bit at a time. As we get to know someone better, we learn whether to hold them at arm's length, draw them closer, or push them away.

I am writing to you about a woman I met at a local community center several months ago. Our paths crossed frequently and we started exchanging pleasantries. Soon enough I noticed she was badmouthing her husband quite a bit.

Within a few weeks of knowing her, she confides in me that she is cheating on her husband. As she had always painted an image of an indifferent and cold husband, I felt sorry for her and wanted to be understanding. My advice to her was do the right thing and leave the marriage if you feel you've found your soul mate.

Thereafter started a pattern of her sharing details about her affair, and before I knew it, I had become a confidante of some sort.

I would often provide her with my insight into why she was doing certain things and also the ramifications of her actions on her kids, if they ever found out. Our conversations would end with her telling me she understood and she felt really good every time she spoke to me.

This continued for a while, and I soon started realizing she always had some excuse not to change things and was relishing sharing details of other men who flirted with her and with whom she flirted back. This made me question whether she even loved the man she was having an affair with.

I started seeing a pretty selfish person who, whatever the justification with her loveless marriage, was intent on playing up her sexuality to boost her self-image.

Lately she has been suggesting our families meet. I am uncomfortable with this whole idea as it would mean I meet her husband and pretend I don't know what his wife is up to. It would also mean my family would get caught up in the charade.

What started off as lending a sympathetic ear to an acquaintance has turned into making me feel I am part of something immoral and wrong. This woman, of course, is very comfortable switching personas and does not seem to suffer guilt pains.

I am uncomfortable with the turn of events and am considering not volunteering at our community center just to avoid crossing paths with her.

-Allison

Allison, she is an exhibitionist. When she watches you squirm or turn red, she's having a party. If she were with your family, knowing someone in the room knows she is cheating and might tell her husband, it would thrill her.

Part of her pleasure comes from parading her behavior and knowing it makes you uncomfortable. She is a lot like swingers. Once they bring up their behavior, you can be sure they are only interested in using you for their own pleasure.

Certain people have a predatory nature, and predators have certain skills. Identifying nice, polite people is one of them. Is this person weaker? Can I use them? Can I control them?

You are a little dumbstruck because this predator is a female, but think about what she is doing. She tells a stranger about her affair and her flirtations, and she has a good time doing it. That tells you she is running under a different set of rules than you are.

The question is how do you battle someone with no morals, low morals, or different morals? Your goal is not to change them, educate them, or inform them. Your goal is to extricate yourself from them.

Because her nature is unpredictable, you need to protect yourself. First, tell your husband and several other people close to you what is going on. Then use the least means possible to get away from her and avoid her.

You don't need to have this environment stolen away from you, but you need to be prepared if she retaliates by lying about you. People like her have more experience than you will ever have in playing this game.

-Wayne & Tamara

One-upmanship is an obvious indicator of a frenemy. One-upmanship is aggressive and expresses the desire to dominate. It is the opposite of friendship.

I desperately need help ending a friendship I know I must end. For the past two years I have given advice to a friend with problems. My friend would call daily to ask for direction on handling situations she seemed unable to deal with. In my willingness to help, I gave her the best information I could based on my experience.

The Friendship Solution

Yesterday, my friend phoned me and during the conversation mentioned she didn't feel I was being honest with myself. She insinuated my husband was probably gay, and that he was either lying to me, lying to himself, or both. This came out of the blue, and I was flabbergasted. She also said she knew her remarks might end our friendship.

I asked her to explain. She said she just "knew" my husband was using me to blend in with society. I should add that she hardly knows my husband, and I have never asked for her advice about my life or my marriage. I defended myself by saying my husband is not a knuckle-dragging, truck-pulling kind of guy, but he is definitely not gay.

She said she was just being honest. I told her honesty is not always called for. You don't tell someone if you think they are ugly! I am still quite shaken by having to defend my husband's sexuality and my honesty. I certainly cannot remain friends with such a person. Please help me end this friendship with finesse.

-Sonya

Sonya, for two years your friend has been the center of attention with her problems. You tried to help, and you tried to be her friend. Now she is ready to end the relationship if she can't gain the upper hand.

Perhaps she is tired of playing the victim and wants to diminish what you have. Perhaps she wants to humiliate and hurt you. Perhaps she has other motives. It doesn't matter. What she said attacks you and your husband.

This situation doesn't call for finesse but for firmness. What you need to do is more like firing a bad employee than talking with a friend. End contact with her. Don't defend yourself or give credence to what she says.

Take her comments for what they are: valueless. Give them no more thought than you would the peel of an orange. Once thrown away, it is never thought of again.

-Wayne & Tamara

Ending a Friendship

When Natalia Lusinski, a journalist, interviewed three therapists for *Business Insider*, they gave her nine reasons for ending a friendship.[3]
1. The friendship is one-sided.
2. The friend betrayed your trust.
3. The friend can't keep a secret.
4. The friend is constantly negative.
5. You have little to talk about.
6. The friend creates too much drama.
7. The friend is passive-aggressive.
8. The friend dismisses your concerns.
9. The friend makes you feel worse, not better.

The question is when we need to end a friendship, how should we do it?

The answer is, there is no one right way.

Some people end friendships cold turkey. They ghost the other party, disappearing without warning or explanation.

Others are more comfortable with a gradual fade out or by becoming hard to reach. Still others search the internet for a solution. WikiHow, for example, has an ending-a-friendship template describing how to end a friendship in nine steps, with pictures.

Still others suggest "we take a break," or they schedule "the talk," laying out reasons why the friendship must end. But there's a problem with these latter two methods. They invite the other party to give counterarguments, promise to change, lay on a guilt trip, get angry, or retaliate.

One woman told us when she tried to end a friendship on the phone, the other person replied, "Nice to know when a friend is down on her luck, you're not there."

Steve Martin and Dan Aykroyd did a comedy routine as two "wild and crazy Czech guys" in patterned shirts and checkered pants. In their "native land" a breakup with a girl was accomplished by saying, "I break with thee, I break with thee, I break with thee. I throw dog poop on your shoes."

We don't recommend that method, but whatever method you use, don't relent.

Sometimes, people you want to defriend can't be avoided. Perhaps they live next door. But if all you can do is correctly categorize where they belong in your life, do that.

There is no place in our lives for people who are rude, insensitive, or hurtful.

I have a question about ending a friendship. I would like to feel I did what I had to do, that I was not just being too sensitive.

The woman in question was a friend of mine for some eight years. We shared a passionate love of horses; it was our common interest. In addition, during our friendship we both had troublesome relationships and helped each other through the worst times.

Some months ago, however, I had photos taken of my horse and I. When I showed them to my friend, she accused me of being vain and basically said my horse was ugly. I stopped talking to her. I was horribly hurt. After several months, I made contact and slowly we resurrected our friendship.

Well, just this week I bought a new horse, a one-year-old Arabian. He is not the most expensive or impressive of his breed, but he is undeniably beautiful. When I showed his photos to my friend, she immediately criticized his appearance and asked if he was even purebred. I said, "Of course, I have paperwork to prove it."

My friend was openly hostile. She ended an email saying my new horse was ugly. She said she did not want to have to say that, that she was initially being polite for the sake of our friendship, but I "forced" her to say it. Her final word was an angry acknowledgment that she is not allowed to use the word "ugly."

When I read that, it seemed to me she is more interested in being right than in keeping me as a friend and saying a real sorry. This is all the more hurtful considering she made it sound like she was the victim.

-Maggie

Ending a Friendship

Maggie, this woman used her spurs on you, and you bucked her off. Bravo! You shouldn't feel bad. She's intentionally cruel. Her remarks were barbed and meant to hurt.

Giving her a second chance allowed her to victimize you again. That's irritating, but you don't need her to acknowledge that you are right. You just need to end this. People like her are always right, especially when they are wrong.

-Wayne & Tamara

The expression everyone deserves a second chance is false. As a general rule, it applies only to children.

I have reconnected with K, a woman I knew years ago. Let's just say K has issues. She wants me to take all her personal and business papers and sort them into three piles: keep, toss, and give away. And she wants me to do this on my own.

Panic attack! K's house is in chaos. If she doesn't know where her papers are, how can I find them? In addition, she boards dogs and keeps them inside because she hasn't built kennels yet. She also has two divorces behind her and big debts.

K lives in the country. She said, "I will call you on a moment's notice when I am ready to come in." But after she called she failed to show. Next day, I learned she ended up getting together with a lady friend and drinking all day.

I told her I would help, but she needs to help me help her. I have a bad feeling about this.

-Ali

Ali, a traditional Girl Scout song says, "Make new friends and keep the old, one is silver and the other gold." But like a lot of clichés this one is full of exceptions.

Twitter and Facebook may make it a snap to reconnect with others, but often they are people we never had much in common with. That doesn't mean friends are unimportant. Just the reverse. Researchers have found having good friends helps us live longer, fight off colds, and be less susceptible to heart attacks.

In one fascinating study researchers led people to the base of a steep hill and fitted them with heavy backpacks.[4] Then they asked them to estimate the steepness of the hill. Those standing without friends judged the hill steeper than those among friends.

But if good friends comfort us, the reverse is also true. K is a badly disorganized person. You can have compassion for her, but staying in her orbit will likely pull you down without lifting her up. A week after you organize her life it will be chaos again, and she will blame you for everything.

We live in an odd age. Researchers often find complicated ways to say what should be obvious. The steepness researchers, for example, concluded that a psychosocial resource, social support, affects the visual perception of geographical slants.

Your grandmother would have said it more simply, along the lines of the Bette Midler song. You gotta have friends. Genuine friends, not the other kind.

-Wayne & Tamara

And finally…

About eight years ago, I first became friends with my college roommate "Cindy." At the time she was dating "John." Our friendship ended shortly before Cindy moved out of our college apartment. In all honesty, I was going through an unhealthy time, and she had her own problems.

Not long after that I got my life back on track, met my future husband, and attended law school. Four years later, I touched base with Cindy. In retrospect, my husband thinks I contacted her because I either subconsciously wanted to show her I was in a good place or wanted closure.

Ending a Friendship

Cindy was now engaged to John. Back in college, people didn't think John was good enough for her, and I thought she was rebelling by dating him. But I grew to see maybe John was more insecure than anything else.

When I introduced my future husband to Cindy and John, he did not like John. John was his usual crass self. He would brag about drinking in college, talk inappropriately about women, and turn any conversation into a story about himself.

When I told my future husband about John's good qualities, he said he was waiting to see them. He didn't want to become friends with John and Cindy, but he made the best of it for my sake. In time, John's behavior started to wear on both of us, and Cindy's faults became more noticeable.

Then John offended me in a whole new way. At our wedding, he met my attorney mentor, a professor at my law school. She agreed to give John advice. When her help fell short of actually getting him in, John told my husband he thought my mentor didn't help at all, and neither had I.

To top it off, when I threw a going-away party for an attorney friend at my house, I invited Cindy and she wanted to bring John. My gut told me John would either irritate or embarrass me in front of my boss, attorney friends, and business contacts.

So I politely asked Cindy to ask John to dress and act conservatively. Mind you, he often dresses in T-shirts with holes, plays with his tongue ring, and flips cigarette butts on the lawn. Cindy and John were offended. I apologized, but inside I was angry. Many times John offended us, but we didn't make an issue out of it.

The next time we saw them Cindy talked to my husband while coldly ignoring me. When I spoke with John, he turned it into an argument and yelled at me in public.

How can I move on so I don't feel angry toward these people?

-Marie

Marie, your husband is likely right. You wanted to show Cindy you had gone somewhere and had a better man than she did.

Everyone in college knew John as an ass, but you pretended he had a silver lining he never showed. If that were true, it would work both ways. When we see someone good, we should suspect they are hiding their bad side. When we can't accept that some people are an ass, and that is their good side, then we spend our lives misjudging others.

If good people go along and don't call others on offensive behavior, how can they say something later on?

Your anger is displaced. You shouldn't have mined your past to make yourself feel good now. Own up to it. Tell your husband, "My bad. Let's bid these two adieu." Then take him to dinner and promise in the future you'll be more careful about dismissing his feelings.

-Wayne & Tamara

The other side to ending a friendship is having someone end their friendship with us. Perhaps it will come as a relief, or perhaps it will make us sad. Either way, others have rights too, including the right to defriend us. When that happens, we must move on, which is the subject of our next chapter.

CHAPTER 14
MOVING ON

"We have fewer friends than we imagine but more than we know."

—Hugo Von Hofmannsthal, librettist

After Val Walker divorced, she took a break from people.

She moved to the Maine coast near a blue heron sanctuary. Four days a week she worked as a case manager for a mental health agency. Three days a week she was on her own. Val lived in a studio apartment in an old sea captain's house, by an apple orchard, with her cat Ivan.

It was a time for reflection, self-imposed solitude, and calm. She was happy.

The writer Carl Sandburg said, "Only those who come to live with loneliness can come to know themselves and life. I go out there and walk and look at the trees and the sky… I sit on a rock or a stump and say to myself, 'Who are you, Sandburg? Where have you been, and where are you going?'"

That's the life Val Walker chose for herself.

She made three friends and lived in Maine more than a decade. Then funding cuts abolished her job, her cat died, and a best friend ghosted her.

She had major surgery. Discharged by the hospital, her ride home cancelled. Val sat in the hospital lobby feverishly dialing phone numbers with no luck. Finally, a friend of a friend agreed to pick her up.

Eventually, Val Walker moved to Boston and wrote the book *400 Friends and No One to Call*.[1] In the book she describes how she turned this personal catastrophe into a community of friends and she offers resources for making friends. The most obvious lesson from the book is that making friends takes time.

When a friend, especially a best friend, leaves our life, we may be bereft. But we must accept that others have a right to end their friendship with us.

Final Goodbye

Eight years ago, I met someone in high school who would turn out to be my best friend. Seth and I are so much alike we literally feel what the other is thinking. We finish each other's sentences. Even with all this, we are different in many ways.

I began dating Seth's best friend a few months after I met Seth and eventually we were engaged to be married. As well as I claim to know him, I never knew Seth was secretly in love with me. The engagement crashed and burned, but it didn't affect my relationship with Seth other than to bring us closer.

Years passed and we grew up.

At one point I became heavily involved in unhealthy things. After months of trying to get through to me, Seth said he could no longer watch me self-destruct. He walked away. That was the worst pain I ever felt in my life.

Eventually I straightened out, married, and moved away. I found Seth by accident surfing the internet one night, and I emailed him. I discovered he was still in college and had a baby. We started emailing every day, trying to "rediscover" each other.

I am married to a wonderful man, and I am recklessly in love with him. Seth respects that and is happy for me.

The problem? Recently Seth emailed me about all his relationship problems. He compares every woman he meets to me, and he claims they do not measure up.

I told him he is being unfair to himself and to these women. What he and I share can never be duplicated, but that doesn't mean he cannot love another person. Love comes in many forms. You never love anyone the same way you loved someone else.

Seth walked away from me once because he couldn't stand to see the way I was living. Is it my time to walk away? I cannot bear the thought I am the cause for all his failed relationships.

-Laurel

Laurel, the writer Anthony Everitt gives an interesting account of the last days of Caesar Augustus, the first Roman emperor. When Augustus was well into his 70s and in failing health, he was worried about who should succeed him.

There were two likely candidates. One was Tiberius, a middle-aged man. The other was Augustus' grandson Agrippa, still in his 20s. Augustus had a soft spot in his heart for Agrippa, but he also knew Agrippa was an angry young man incapable of leading Rome. In fact, Augustus had exiled him to the small island of Pianosa.

A few months before his death, Augustus secretly went to Pianosa to visit Agrippa. Grandfather and grandson had a joyous reunion. Augustus assured Agrippa of his love and told him that he would soon call him back to Rome. Augustus then returned to his ship, but not before arranging for the young man to be executed.

You never looked at Seth as he looked at you. You saw him almost asexually, even as he made you his Helen of Troy, his Marilyn Monroe, his Charlize Theron. The relationship got stuck there.

Helping Seth maintain his fixation isn't good for you, your husband, or your marriage. It isn't good for Seth. Let him know that the thing which would make you lovers is absent for you. Then break off all contact.

Like Augustus, you are faced with a painful decision. Augustus made his decision to avoid a bloody war of succession. You must make yours for the same reason Seth once walked away from you.

-Wayne & Tamara

Life Lessons

Over the past 15 months, I became close to two girls, "Abby" and "Jenna." We were like the Three Musketeers, emailing each other every single day, writing letters, exchanging phone numbers, always encouraging each other.

About a month ago, Abby started to grow distant and then suddenly started to ignore both me and Jenna with absolutely no explanation at all. Jenna and I tried repeatedly to ask for an explanation but received nothing. It seems Abby replaced the two of us with a group of cooler and more popular girls.

That's not my big problem. It hurts, but it's happened to me before and I'm trying to move on with relative success. However, Jenna is having a much worse time.

Anyway, it's gotten to the point where this whole Abby disaster has made things really bad for Jenna. I finally convinced her to talk to her parents about seeing a counselor and she's now meeting with one, I guess about once a month.

I'm never going to leave Jenna. I truly love and care about her. I want her to be happy, but she's obsessed with getting Abby back. All she does is talk about Abby.

I don't understand why. Abby has shown zero interest in being friends even when I wrote her a letter as if the whole falling out thing was my fault. She ignored every single attempt at communication with us. It's as if we never met.

So I'm really hurt right now by both Abby and Jenna. I'm hurt by Abby because I know I did nothing wrong to offend her, and she abandoned me when I was going through a hard time and needed someone to talk to.

But I'm hurt worse by Jenna because I stay up until 1:00 a.m. every single night talking to her until she goes to bed. I encourage her, I pray for her, I talk to her about whatever she needs or wants to talk about. And all she cares about is Abby.

-Bronwyn

Bronwyn, Alexander Graham Bell said, "We often look so long and regretfully upon the closed door that we do not see the ones which open."

Patterns of thought can be circular, like water going down a drain. When that happens, what we need is less thought and more action. Jenna needs something to work on and something to achieve.

How do you find friends? Usually through a shared something. It can be your neighborhood, school, work, hobby group, basketball practice, volunteer work, or clarinet lessons. Anything. You can meet someone with shared interests in all those places and gain knowledge and self-esteem through improving yourself.

The better person you are, the more diverse and interesting, the more you are attractive to others. Ask, What would it take for me to be one of those people who walks into a room and lights it up? Perhaps you will never quite become that person, but asking the question points you in the right direction.

Every moment spent contemplating the one who moved on is a waste. Nothing you or Jenna can do will change Abby. She is neither a bird in a cage nor an indentured servant. What has Abby done? Taken her life in her hands and steered it in another direction with resolve.

Life always changes, especially when we are young. Wait until one of you has a boyfriend.

First and foremost remember it is your life to live. If you are not living it and directing it, then you have given it to others. That's why older people sometimes ask themselves, How did I get here and not where I wanted to be?

Jenna can't relive the glory days when you were all friends. That's looking at the closed door when so many others are open.

-Wayne & Tamara

There are situations that are inexplicable, though we are desperate for an answer. The best thing to do is to let them go.

I have a coworker I've been friendly with for several years. About three months ago, she started being too busy to have lunch together. I asked her once whether anything was wrong and whether I offended her in some way. She assured me nothing was amiss and she considers me a friend at work.

But in the past month she stopped speaking to me unless absolutely necessary. No more sailing into my office, flopping onto a chair, and asking, "How is life?" No more talking about her work stuff and home stuff. No more good morning or good night, even when she is leaving the office next door to mine and always used to pop her head in.

Once she went so far as to look through me to say good morning to someone else. Another time she was in the conference room having arrived first for a meeting. I arrived second, and she kept her head down as if very busy until a third person arrived, then she said hello to both of us.

There have been hundreds of instances of not seeming to hear me when I say a normal pleasant greeting to her in her office or in the hallway. I feel hurt and disturbed as I wonder if I'm being accused of something I didn't do, or if I put my foot in my mouth in a way that never struck me as offensive.

I feel it would be useless to ask again if something is wrong. I think my real question is, how can I make myself tougher so a thing like this doesn't occupy my mind and bring me close to tears a few times every day? Are there steps a person can take to grow a tougher skin?

-Alexia

Alexia, Wayne once asked a 60-ish friend why he was always in such high spirits. This friend explained as a young man he worried incessantly. He worried over tests, dates, and whether he would find a job. Then, in his late teens, he had an epiphany. Worry accomplishes nothing.

What you need is not so much a tougher skin as to stop worrying over things beyond your control. You asked if there was a problem and she denied it. You've done all you can. For some reason, the friendly woman with an office next door moved away and a person with whom you have little in common and no rapport moved in. That's curious, but it's not a reason for worry.

In the personal space between her ears something is going on. You are likely never to know what. Wayne once smiled at a friend on a street corner and was baffled when a woman he didn't know and hadn't noticed crossed the street to ask why he was laughing at her.

People do all manner of strange things. People tell tales, create hoopla, and use passive aggression. They also show extraordinary kindness and care. Good people torture themselves asking why, why, why. But the answer is often as simple as displaced emotion.

Not everything in life carries the same weight. Your family carries a certain weight, your partner a certain weight, your house a certain weight, and your neighbors a certain weight. Your job carries a certain weight. You are giving her too much weight. Your purpose at work is work.

Treat this woman with the normal corporate politeness used in the workplace. Treat her professionally, clinically, and distantly. When you walk into a room and she is there, ignore her, but with a third person present act normally.

It always helps to ask ourselves, What is my purpose in life? Then let your life proceed from your purpose and not from the oddities and quirks of others.

-Tamara

When we are lonely, we need to realize how big the world is. We have true friends are out there somewhere, and by engaging in life we will find them.

James Boswell remarked, "We cannot tell the precise moment when friendship is formed. As in filling a vessel drop by drop, there is at last a drop which makes it run over; so in a series of kindnesses there is at last one which makes the heart run over."

Perhaps Jeffrey Hall, a communications professor at the University of Kansas, took Boswell's comment as a challenge. Hall is the man who tried to determine exactly how much clock time it takes to make a friend.[2]

Jeffrey Hall conducted a study with two parts. In the first part, he analyzed an online survey of adults who had relocated in the past six months. He asked these people to think of someone they met since the move and discuss how the relationship moved forward. Hall was especially interested in what the two shared in closeness, activities, and hours spent together.

In the second part of his study, Hall tracked 112 new freshmen at the University of Kansas. These young people were asked to name two people they met since starting school. Weeks later, Hall followed up to see how the friendships were progressing, and he categorized the friendships in four ways: acquaintance, casual friend, friend, and close friend.

The results from both studies were similar. Jeffrey Hall found it takes 40 – 60 hours together to move from acquaintance to casual friend, 80 – 100 hours to become friends, and more than 200 hours to become good friends.

Hall also found the amount of time since a first meeting doesn't predict the growth of friendship. As he said, "It is possible to know someone for years, but not develop a friendship, and to know someone for six weeks and become best friends." He added, "You can't snap your fingers and make a friend."

When we lose a friend, or find ourselves without friends, it is a call to action and a call to live a wider life. It can also be a call to understand our problem.

I have a question I am hoping you can help answer. It seems all my life, almost all my friends I've made have gradually fallen away from me. What can I do to not have this happen?

Here's a basic rundown of the story. I thought my high school friends were awesome, and I saw myself keeping in contact for the rest of our lives. I went away for college while most of them stayed in state. I tried to keep in contact with them.

Most of the time I did not get much of a response, but I thought, Whatever, maybe they're busy.

I'm back home for summer from my first year of college, which kicked ass. I made a new group of great friends, and I was hoping I could meet up with some of my old high school friends. I tried to organize a casual get-together and invited them all.

But the night comes around and nobody showed up. I thought, Whatever, maybe they're busy.

I run into them at a classmate's wedding. Now, just to clarify, I'm not arrogant enough to think my get-together is as important as my classmate's wedding. I was just happy to see them. But my point is I tried to talk to them to see how they were doing, and they all gave me short, curt responses, or none at all.

They stuck to themselves most of the night and talked about what they were going to do, as a group, afterwards and the next day. I made it obvious I perked my ears up, but they snubbed me.

I was hurt. I wondered, What happened? If I hadn't seen a friend in a year, I would totally want to see how they were and what was going on with their lives. But I thought, If they're going to act like that, forget them. I made friends in college that were awesome and I'd see them when I got back in the fall.

To make an equally long story short, pretty much the exact same thing happens when I get back to college. My friends, who only a few months ago were so dear to me, suddenly decide to leave me out of their happenings.

At first I thought they were too busy when they didn't reply to me, but then I'd see them all hanging out together in the cafeteria or at events. All of them except me.

I get out of college and into the "real" world, and, well, it's pretty much the same story. This has become a recurring theme in my life…

-Kinsley

Some people know they lack social skills. Many others lack social skills and don't know it.

A basic sign of poor social skills is difficulty getting along with others.

Chris Segrin, a behavioral scientist of the University of Arizona, conducted a survey to measure social skills.[3] When he recruited a nationally representative sample of 775 people, aged 18 to 91, he found a link between poor social skills and poorer physical and mental health.

As Segrin explains, "People with poor social skills have high levels of stress and loneliness in their lives."[4] He likens loneliness to the feeling people get when they can't find their keys. "When we lose our keys, 99% of the time we find them, the stress goes away, we get in the car and it's over."

But Segrin says, "Lonely people experience that same sort of frantic search—in this case, not for car keys but for meaningful relationships—and they don't have the ability to escape from that stress."

Social skills fall broadly into four categories.
- Ability to provide emotional support to others
- Ability to share personal information
- Ability to stand up to unreasonable requests
- Ability to introduce yourself to others and get to know them

The good news, Segrin says, is social skills can be learned. For some, the first step might be getting a book or visiting an online forum or website. But Segrin suggests, "For people who really want to improve their social skills and work on them, there's therapy, there's counseling, and there is social skills training."

Social skills are learned over time, starting with our family of origin. Unfortunately, the family of origin is commonly the main cause of poor social skills.

While building social skills is beyond the scope of this book, if you suspect that might be your problem making friends, this is an area to dig into.

Sometimes when we are forced to end a relationship, the other person retaliates…

My mother is in a nursing home. She is lucid but cannot get around easily. I visit twice a week and pay two women to keep her company on the other days. One woman became ill and so I put the word out on Facebook that I was looking for a replacement.

A friend recommended a friend of hers, Joan. I didn't know Joan well, but she lives in my neighborhood and we have mutual acquaintances.

About three months into the job, I discovered Joan was talking about me behind my back. She felt my mother was being treated poorly and I wasn't sticking up for her. I was stunned. We did have a problem with one caregiver; however, when I reported the problem to the head nurse, he took care of it immediately.

This home is accredited, has an above average rating and a reputation to protect. Friends in healthcare recommended it and colleagues of mine have parents there as well. For the most part, my mother says she is happy. When she's not, I listen and ask for adjustments.

Joan's criticism made me uneasy and a few days later, while I was still processing it, she visited my mother and found her unconscious. My mother naps after lunch, and when Joan visited, she couldn't rouse her. Instead of reporting it, Joan waited until after she'd left the home to tell me.

Panicked phone calls and chaos ensued.

I suspected Joan of wanting to teach me and the staff a lesson, but I'm still not clear what anyone gained by her irresponsible behavior.

I let her go a few days later and told her it was because my mother's health had deteriorated. There is some truth to this, but it's not the whole story. However, given Joan's lack of discretion and flair for drama, I felt the less said the better.

Despite this, she went to my mother's nursing home a few days ago and asked my mother why she'd been let go. When my mother didn't know how to answer, Joan turned on the companion who was there at the time. Both were upset.

I called Joan, and when the call went to voicemail, I left a message telling her not to visit again. I said I didn't understand why she found the situation confusing when I had given her a clear explanation. I know Joan has had some hard knocks in life but that does not make her behavior any more acceptable.

Joan's version of things had already been circulating for a few weeks by the time I heard of it. Now I sense discomfort among our mutual friends. I suspect Joan is characterizing me as a heartless daughter and it's just not true.

-Caroline

Caroline, why is Joan widely disseminating her tale of woe? For two reasons. She is embarrassed about being fired and she wants to get her version of events out there first.

Often people like Joan go through an entire social circle before everyone learns what she is like. The normal rule is the first person to tell a lie is believed, while the second person—who tells the truth—is discounted. Our brains shouldn't work that way but they do.

What should you do now? Go to the nursing home and bar this woman from seeing your mother. With your acquaintances, leave the matter alone unless it comes up.

If it comes up, explain you feel sorry for Joan but people take being let go very badly. It wasn't working out; you are sorry it affects her financial situation and that she is upset.

The tack to take is, "As with any personal care situation, there has to be a good fit. There wasn't and I feel bad about it." With everyone exude the idea, "I was in the right, but I feel bad she feels bad."

-Wayne & Tamara

Let us amplify that answer.

At one time Elbert Hubbard was one of the most widely quoted people on the planet. In *The Motto Book*, published in 1907, he wrote, "Never explain—your friends do not need it and your enemies will not believe you anyhow."

Unfortunately, that's not quite right. Two 17th century philosophers, Descartes and Spinoza, had something to say on this issue. Descartes claimed when people hear something, they pause and weigh the evidence before deciding what to believe. Spinoza thought that was nonsense. He believed most of the time people believe the first thing they hear.

Modern psychology is inclined to agree with Spinoza. That is why, if you think you might be victimized by someone spreading a false story, it pays to get your version of events out there first. However, if you feel confident people know your character, you might say nothing.

The problem is false narratives can come back to haunt you, and toxic people will say anything. That's why you should be prepared when they employ emotional blackmail, retaliation, or lies.

I had a close friend that I connected with unlike anyone else. After he mentioned his online webpage one night, I followed up with an email asking when he would add me to his list of friends. His reply was a vicious message confirming he kept me separate from his other friends. He said I was "unhealthy" to ask to be included on the list.

I felt like a leper. He went weird on me after a lovely time where we could talk about anything. Now I have anxiety about leaving my house since his world and my world are the same place. I sent him an email asking for an explanation, respect, sensitivity, anything—and was ignored.

This could have ended with me being upset after a respectful explanation, yet he chose a traumatic reply. I've been to counseling and was told to confront this man as his behavior is strange and deserves an explanation. But my message was ignored, and now I feel a sense of shame.

How do I get answers from such an illogical situation?

-Deanna

Deanna, counseling is not a passkey which unlocks every relationship. What your counselor didn't tell you is that while you are free to want to know why, he is free not to tell you. Some people end a relationship with silence; some people end it with cruelty; some people end it with reasons. People will do what people will do.

A friendship is no more than an invitation to trade. It is not a guarantee of anything. A relationship ending badly is common, and the injured party often seeks an answer. If you wanted to end your relationship with this man, you might count on the same right not to explain yourself. But with the shoe on the other foot, you demand an explanation.

All you need now is the ability to pass this man in a hallway without feeling embarrassed. That is something within the limits of what counseling can do.

-Wayne & Tamara

No Explanation Necessary
Last year, I abruptly ended a relationship with my next-door neighbor because she used me as a convenience and did not treat me as a friend. Six months ago, she sent a card explaining that she did not understand why I no longer talked to her. I did not respond.

Now she has employed the use of mutual acquaintances to get to me. I have not addressed this to them because, quite frankly, it didn't involve them. Unfortunately, now it does. How do I address this without coming off as the "bad guy"?

-Connie

Connie, if your ultimate concern is what other people think, you are always going to lose because you don't control the thoughts of others. Whatever baggage, home life, and previous experience in this world they have will determine what they feel about you. Since you cannot change their beliefs, ideas, or experiences, you cannot determine how they will feel about anything they come into contact with.

A person you don't hold in high regard or wish to have contact with has now decided to enlist others to get what she wants. You took away her ability to use you, so she is now using others to get what she is being denied.

If you are concerned what these mutual acquaintances think, you are going to put yourself under the control of others again. But if you wish to have your own life and exercise your rights as an individual on this planet, you must put how you feel about yourself, and your actions, first.

Simply tell those acquaintances, despite what this neighbor may have told them, you've made it clear you do not wish to have contact with her.

Make it clear you are under no obligation to explain why. If we wish to be free to have our own likes, friendships, and pursuits, then we can't allow others to impose their likes over ours. Any explanation you give will only elicit argument and debate over your rights.

This is not a debate. This is your life, and this is your right. Users, abusers, and controllers do not take no for an answer. If you let them tie you up in justifying yourself, then they have succeeded.

-Wayne & Tamara

The last three letters touch on anger, envy, and jealousy, the subject of our next chapter.

CHAPTER 15
JEALOUSY

"Whenever a friend succeeds, a little something in me dies."[1]
— Gore Vidal, novelist

I just got hired at my company and my coworker/close friend did not. She got passed over and remains a temp. She has not spoken to me in a week.

She claims it was because I didn't tell her I was getting hired, even though company policy states I couldn't until it was official. When I did try to tell her, she refused to speak with me. It was then I learned she heard it from someone else.

I've bent over backwards for this woman and now she won't even look at me. Am I wrong if I wait for her to approach me? I'm so angry at the situation I don't think I should apologize.

-Renae

Renae, you can't apologize to someone who snubs you because of your good fortune. You know, and we know, she isn't angry because you didn't tell her; she is angry because you got the job and she didn't.

Any overture to this woman will make her think you were wrong and she is entitled to be in the superior position. It will tell her you condone her actions.

You can't do that. Friends want good things for each other; they aren't spiteful. Without a full-on, meaningful apology from her, she doesn't need to be in your life. We have to be careful who we call "friend."

-Wayne & Tamara

When Gore Vidal said that a friend's success made something in him die, he echoed a line from Aeschylus. "It is in the character of very few men to honor without envy a friend who has prospered."

But is that the whole story?

It seems more likely that feelings of envy and jealousy arise in people who don't like where they are in life. When we envy others, it is often not because of what they have but because they trigger feelings of hopelessness and self-loathing in us, though at such a subtle level we don't know why we dislike them.

Friendship itself does not beget jealousy; a jealous person has that quality within them.[1] Often a person is more than jealous, they are possessive.

In the television show *Billions*, a story about rivalries at a hedge fund, Mike "Wags" Wagner repeats the prayer he said as a child. "Now I lie me down to sleep, I pray the Lord my soul to keep, and if I die before I wake, I pray that all my toys should break … so my brother and sister can't play with them."

And finally, there are those who think, *My station in life is where it ought to be, slightly above your station.* But if you rise above me, something is wrong. That's neither jealousy nor envy. It is simply egotism.

Sometimes good people mislabel what they are feeling as jealousy. They blame themselves for the feeling, but it is not jealousy they feel.

For the past two years I have been in a wonderful, committed relationship with a great woman and it keeps getting better. When we first started seeing each other, she was seeing someone else.

While she initially downplayed the importance of that relationship, I came to learn it was more serious than she led me to believe. This man still contacts her frequently in hopes they can resume where they left off.

She replies to him when he emails asking how her life is going, and she gives him enough information about where she will be that he shows up to plead his case. She assures me he means nothing to her and is committed to our relationship. I believe her.

Here's my problem. Despite how great everything is, I find myself tormented by thoughts of the two of them together. I fantasize about confronting her or spend hours thinking about confronting him.

So far I've been able to keep these irrational feelings to myself for the most part. I never thought of myself as the jealous type, and I have no similar feelings about anyone she was with prior to us dating.

In your articles on jealousy you take a pretty hard line, saying it is more about power and control than love and it is the jealous partner's issue to deal with. I agree with that intellectually.

My question is, how can I make these irrational feelings and tormenting thoughts go away? They are making me miserable. Several times I have come close to saying things I know I would regret.

-Robert

Robert, psychologists believe human beings have two systems of reasoning. One system is rule-based and rational while the other is associative and emotional.

Both systems yield results. The main difference between the two is that one system gives results expressed in feelings, while the other gives results plus a line of reasoning.

Most of us, of course, look at this in simpler terms. Some things we know in our mind, other things we feel in our gut. Intuitively we know that the most reliable guide to action occurs when both systems agree.

You see your distress as a clash between rational thought (I shouldn't be jealous) and irrational feelings (but I am). We disagree. We think you've come to a conclusion you would rather not face.

Your partner dated you and another man. Fair enough. We understand how that could happen early in a relationship. But, and it's a big but, she continues to tell this other man what she is doing and where she will be doing it.

This man is not a friend. He is a past lover ardently pursuing her. She is enabling him. Your rational mind has drawn a reasonable conclusion: beware.

And your other system of reasoning, feelings? Well, feelings evolved for a simple reason: to give us a quick answer to a problem. Are they always right? No. But in a healthy person they can be as reliable as reasoning.

Your emotional warning system went off for good reason. Your gut knows her behavior is wrong, just as your mind reasons it is wrong.

We don't see you as a jealous man. Instead we see both systems of reasoning in agreement. This "great woman" is acting in a way inconsistent with being in a "wonderful and committed" relationship.

She says he's nothing to her, but she knows it's not nothing to him, and she knows it's not nothing to you.

Why are you biting your tongue? Because you fear if you confront her she will leave and go to the other man. It's time for a conversation with your girlfriend, a conversation which will determine if this relationship has a future.

-Wayne & Tamara

As Robert said, our position on jealousy is simple. Never put up with it. Never go along with it. Never placate it.

Close to the Vest
I'm 40 and dating again, which is confusing stuff. My friend tells me the man I have been dating for three weeks is moving too slow. I disagree. We've had two dates in three weeks with the promise of him fixing me dinner next time. He calls every three or four days, and we chat for an hour or so. There have been nice hugs and kisses at the end of dates.

We are both self-employed and work 60 hours plus each week. I feel he is interested and we have a great time together, but my other single friends tell me he isn't interested because he hasn't yet tried to have sex with me. So what do you think? Taking his time or not interested? Oh yes, he's done all the calling and asking out.

-Sara

Sara, you neglected to mention option three. Your single friend is jealous. A nice man, a gentleman who is not rushing you ... and there's something wrong?

Share fewer details with your girlfriend, keep more within your own heart, and see what develops...

-Tamara

Listen to how the next writer describes her "best friend."

My boyfriend and I have been dating for a couple of years. He's my best friend and I love him. However, recently I've been putting a strain on our relationship because I'm envious of his successes and his skills.

As far as he's concerned, there's no reason for me to be jealous of him. We're both broke 20-somethings in a similar place in life, so usually we can find comfort in commiserating with each other.

But I'm jealous of his knack for making friends, I'm jealous that he likes his job and I hate mine, and I'm jealous of his enthusiasm for so many things in life. Sometimes when he talks about having fun with his coworkers or being praised for something, I feel so jealous I want to cry. I feel pathetic in comparison.

I don't want him to stop telling me good things in his life. Really, when I'm not upset, I'm proud of him and I want the world to recognize how great he is. Besides, I feel he should be able to tell his own girlfriend about things that make him happy.

I don't always get jealous, but when I do, I get mean and resentful. It makes both of us feel awful. I know this is my own problem, not his, but how do I stop being eaten up with envy? And how can I ask for his support in a constructive way when I'm feeling down about myself, without making it a competition between us?

-Pippa

Pippa, great. You've taken the first step. We praise you for that. You recognize this is your problem and that is the truth, because you would be this way with anyone.

Where you go off track is asking for his support when you feel down about yourself. You don't need to be coddled. You need to focus on, *What am I doing to change this?*

What is envy? "He has this and this and this, and I don't. I see what someone else has, and instead of doing something about it, I feel sorry for myself." That is why we say envy is the easy way out.

First, act as if you have the power to change. Acting powerless will make you powerless and acting miserable will make you miserable.

Second, identify your problems. What concrete, observable, action steps do you need to take to change?

Are you doing anything to improve your work situation? It's not fun to be a broke 20-something, but can you get a better job? Or can you decide to be the best employee until you get that better job? Becoming a high performer will make you feel better about yourself, even in a job you don't like and want to leave.

Observe how your boyfriend and others make friends. Can you use them as your model? Can you see what you might be doing wrong? Imitate others in the things you admire.

Your logical mind and your kind heart want to share in his successes and happiness, but your lower self is trying to drag up this parasitic, relationship-killing envy. Envy is like a dog that won't stop digging holes in your backyard. Accomplishment and personal change are the only things that will stop it.

In asking for his support, you ask to make him complicit in whiny feelings. He cannot comply because then you will feel you have a right to those feelings.

Over and over we tell people the only person they have power to change is themselves. You have a choice. Be with him and change yourself or find someone who has nothing you can envy.

-Wayne & Tamara

Sometimes there is a duality in friendship that can't be resolved because one party has chosen a path which is inconsistent with being the other person's friend.

I've been friends with "Jenny" for three years after my husband and I started a business with her husband. When her husband decided he didn't want to come to work anymore, we pretty much took his name off the business, and they stopped calling and coming over.

We would call, but they'd never answer or return our calls. Through another friend we learned they split up. I had some information about Jenny's husband I thought she needed to know, so I met with her. I told Jenny her husband cheated enough for an entire football team.

Jenny told me she never called because her husband said we didn't pay him an even share of the business profits. Even though we didn't have to, we showed her proof we paid him right. After all that we became friends again. We hung out every other day and talked on the phone every morning.

Jenny even found a guy to like her and her two kids. She seemed really happy and, believe me, if you knew her, a piece of chocolate would make her happier than she ever was in her marriage. The only thing is, she dumped the new guy. Then suddenly she stopped calling and coming over.

Yesterday, I went to her house and her ex was there. I turned around and left. I'm pretty sure the only reason she wants to be with him is because he is the father of her kids, but she is willing to give up her friendship with me for him. I know what you're thinking, same as my husband; she never really was my friend if she would do this.

I wrote her a letter in hopes of getting my friend back, but I'm not sure it will do any good. What else, if anything, should I do?

-Tara

Tara, what your husband said is not quite right. It isn't that Jenny never was your friend; it's that you can't root for both teams in a basketball game. Jenny was faced with two competing realities. Either her husband is a good person worthy of respect or her husband is untrustworthy.

While Jenny was with you she could cast her marriage in one light, but once she went back to him, she had to recast her marriage in a different light. She couldn't hold both pictures in her mind at the same time.

Your experience is a familiar one. Often when a couple breaks up, a friend of one of them will share in all the secrets of the marriage. If the couple gets back together, that friend will be left out in the cold because they know too much. That is what happened to you.

While Jenny's husband is in her life, she cannot be your friend.

-Wayne & Tamara

We have a final word about the diverging paths of friends…

A Friendly Game

I complain a lot and it runs in the family. My close friend made a comment to that effect while at my home Christmas Day for dinner. She also seemed annoyed that I got a better job shortly after being laid off.

I am a successful professional while she is a stay-at-home mom. There has always been a little competitiveness because I am more educated and have an outgoing personality. Yet she is the nicest person I know. She is strong and resilient and has raised her children well and helped me in parenting my kids.

She luckily married her high school sweetheart and they seem happy, whereas I am divorced and unlucky in love. Two of her kids are autistic and she never complains. She is fierce! I love her as a person and hate to think sharing my highs and lows is burdensome to her.

My question, how much is too much sharing? How can one share success without appearing to be gloating, or share difficulties without being a burden?

I find as I get older I am grateful for so many things. I am lucky career-wise, but life still throws curveballs, and I would like to share them.

-Kara

Kara, we look at good conversation as a noncompetitive game of tug-of-war. You get to pull some as the other person gives. Then they get to pull some as you give. The goal is to maintain the flag in the middle, between the pullers, rather than to pull the other person over the line.

That way, when the game ends, everyone feels good. If you don't play that way, there are winners and losers. That's what makes you feel bad; that's what makes them feel bad.

Let the other person have a turn, so they can vent and see you are really listening. Perhaps it's a complaint about a job and you know for a fact they aren't going to quit and aren't going to take classes to get a different job.

Whether we are in a high position or a low position, we all have things we could complain about. We don't work in the world with only good people or diligent people or kind people. There is some turmoil in life no matter where we find ourselves.

But when we realize we have conversed poorly or selfishly, a simple apology ("I'm sorry I talked your ear off" or "You are so kind to listen to me as I go on and on") will make the listener know you appreciate them and are concerned about them.

Your friend is a stay-at-home mom and doesn't participate in the world the same way you do. She could be harboring unfulfilled dreams. Her choices, like all our choices, involve pluses and minuses. You can't know her mind.

We once heard a person call an idea crazy only to have another person (someone with a mentally ill family member) unload the full fury of their wrath and hurt. And we've heard others speak of children as the greatest joy in life to childless couples.

So we suggest, think of good talk as a noncompetitive game of tug-of-war which leaves everyone feeling good.

-Wayne & Tamara

At times, the stakes in maintaining a friendship involve genuine peril.

CHAPTER 16
DANGEROUS FRIENDS

"My name is Death: the last best friend am I."
—Robert Southey, writer

Ten years ago, I became friends with the mother of one of my son's friends. We are both single mothers. Over the years we became good friends and told each other the good, the bad, and the ugly. Until recently we shared a paper route for some extra money.

A few months ago, she changed. Every conversation would start out fine but end with her screaming at me. I don't let her have any opinions; I always put her and her kids down, et cetera. Her son and mine talk on speaker phone, so I hear everything at her house. She has been volatile with her two kids as well.

I became so tired of ending every conversation with one of us in tears I stopped calling. I suspected she was back with her abusive, violent ex, and possibly using again. I know at one point her kids were placed in foster care; he went to jail, she got clean, and the kids were returned.

This man has spent time in jail for kidnapping and torture, drugs, and gang-related charges. A few weeks ago, while our sons were talking, a man's voice came in the background swearing and yelling at her son that "You have to respect me, you little bastard." I could hear things being thrown.

I've had run-ins with him before and he knows I encouraged her not to be with him. I care about her and her kids and am scared for them. I am also so angry at her that she would put her family at risk.

Pushing me away probably was a way to cover him being back. My attempts to contact her family were ignored. Her mother left me a voicemail saying I do not need to concern myself.

Friends of mine know this family. They encouraged me to contact her social worker. They have already done so but were told since all the information is coming from me, I will have to call. I've already gotten the social worker's number but have not called.

Another option is contacting her father, a retired police officer who owns the home she lives in. He would not tolerate the ex living there. I do not have his number but can get it.

Should I call the social worker? Should I call the father? Should I confront her directly? Or do all three?

My conscience will not allow me to walk away when I know these people are in danger. I know these kids. They are so angry at their father. I don't want to damage their lives any more than has already been done, but I have to do something.

-Brianna

Brianna, you can't let this go because you think you have the power to make this situation what you want it to be. But you don't have that power. In your head you see only rosy outcomes, but there is no certainty any outcome will be rosy.

If the children are taken away and put in foster care, will they thank you? No. If you confront this woman, will she thank you? No. Will her ex-husband thank you? No. He's a violent man. The only thanks you might get from him will be late at night when he drops by your house to "thank you" in person.

Your conscience asks a nagging question. *What will happen if I don't intervene?* Instead you should focus on what will happen if you do intervene. Don't put yourself and your family at risk.

This woman has made her choices. If you think intervention won't backfire on you and your son, tell her social worker. In any event, keep your son away from these people and let the rest go.

Your son can learn compassion, but first he needs to learn about danger, and you need to realize you can't help someone who does not want your help. This situation requires professional intervention.

-Wayne & Tamara

It makes us slightly crazy when people refuse to respect danger.

A new couple, renters, moved in across the street two years ago. My husband and I quickly became friends and hangout buddies with them. Both are heavy drinkers, and though neither my husband nor I drink, we somehow managed to have fun together playing board games and video games.

We sold our house and built a new one a block away. The couple who bought the house turned out to be nasty, threatening people, and they had buyer's remorse. As soon as they bought the house, their finances went downhill, and when the housing market crashed, selling the house for what they paid was no longer an option.

Needless to say, they resented us. After they were drunk one night and firing guns, we talked to a lawyer about getting a restraining order. Our friends continued to be great, however, until the wife got obsessed with my husband and me. If we invited other friends to dinner, she would get mad.

Her husband travels and she only behaves this way while he is gone. Over time she began drinking more, and her behavior grew worse. Though we had been close friends, when she started playing manipulative games, I backed off.

I wasn't trying to end it, just redefining and changing the dynamics. She told someone we were shunning her. Actually, we never said or did anything mean, disrespectful, or inconsiderate.

Last week, she told me, with satisfaction, she had become friends with the crazy, threatening people who bought our house. She hangs out with them every day. In one way, we feel relieved to be rid of her; in another, we feel in danger because her behavior is so unpredictable we don't know what she is capable of.

Her husband is still nice, and we doubt he is aware of her odd conduct. In a weird way, we feel we've lost friends who were fun to be with. For now, though, we can't walk into our front yard without being stared at by this woman because she sits on her porch all the time.

She sent me an email and the subject was "Items." It said she would appreciate it if I would return the books and cat carrier she loaned me. How should we handle this?

-Helen

Helen, stop saying this couple was fun to hang out with. Having fun went out the window as soon as you had reason to fear this woman.

Once her behavior changed, it was as if she was juggling a hand grenade in front of you and you didn't know if she might pull the pin. Now that she is hanging out with the troublesome people who bought your house, the danger is she might aim them at you just like a gun.

Playing Pollyanna is dangerous. We need to have the full range of behavior at our disposal all the time. We must be prepared to treat good people one way and unstable or dangerous people another way.

Return the books and the cat carrier posthaste. Make of your home a safety zone. Reading about personal safety and consulting with local law enforcement would be a good first step.

-Wayne & Tamara

Danger has one name but many forms…

I have been dating a man named Cal for the past six months. We are very close and treat each other extremely well. We talk frequently about a long-term future. I couldn't ask for things to be better.

But there is one major problem. Cal's ex-girlfriend repeatedly interferes in our relationship. She is what you would call a psycho. Almost every weekend *we go out to clubs and then to an after bar party. When we are out, we run into her and she picks fights with us. We have had drinks thrown in our faces.*

Once, I turned around to say something to her, and she kicked me in the head. I fell down a flight of stairs. She was two stairs above me when I turned, so it might have been an accident. She has also broken into our house and smashed a window. Cal tells her to leave us alone but she won't.

She phones here every week. Cal will say things like, "I still love you, but I'm not in love with you." However, she is not the kind of person who understands that concept. She has made me a very angry person. If this continues, I may walk away from this relationship. That would be giving into her, but I don't know what else to do.

-Talena

Talena, when you are involved with a stalker, the only solution is to cut them off. There is no middle ground. When property damage and physical assault are involved, things are more than annoying. They are dangerous.

Cutting off the stalker means hanging up the phone, changing phone numbers, and not going where they go. Each time Cal talks to this woman, she has succeeded in extending their relationship. When he says, "I love you, but I'm not in love you," all she hears is "I love you."

At this point, the ball is in Cal's court. If he doesn't end this relationship, part of him wants it to continue.

-Wayne

At times, the danger is to a person the writer cares about...

I have a friend I consider to be like a little sister. She is 16 and recently started seeing a 22-year-old. I vaguely know this guy because we are second or third cousins. I don't want to lose her as a friend, but I want her to understand age difference is a big deal and people around her are not blowing it out of proportion.

She is not being unreasonable or getting upset with me, but I think that is because all I said is I don't really approve. I don't want to get too caught up in her personal decisions and lose her as a friend. What can I do to explain why a six-year age difference is a problem now but wouldn't be if she were older?

-Sigrid

Sigrid, there is an old saying that you can always tell a Harvard man, but you can't tell him much. Parents of teenagers know exactly what that means. Even teens who acknowledge folly in others remain stuck in the folly of "bad things can't happen to me."

Just as there is a difference between playing to win and playing not to lose, so there is a difference between big sister and friend. Big sister expresses a familial connection, which allows one to step over bounds at times. It also means don't bring disgrace to us or harm the family.

Friendship is more laissez-faire. It implies the other person is free to make their own mistakes as long as it doesn't hurt the friend. If you play not to lose this girl's friendship, you can't protect her. Standing back, in effect, consents to what she does.

Though your friend may be flattered by interest from an adult male, there is a vast difference between 16 and 22 in brain development, socialization, sexuality, and life experience. The law understands this and so do the norms of society.

Tell this girl, in your own words, the dangers you foresee. It is better to play big sister because, if you don't speak up and something bad happens, you will feel responsible.

-Wayne & Tamara

Megan Gunnar, a child psychologist at the University of Minnesota, has a wonderful way of describing the position this 16-year-old is in.

Gunnar explains that until puberty, parents provide the mental scaffolding a child needs. After that, she says, parents are "not in your hypothalamus anymore. They've moved out of your body."[1]

While her parents may have moved out of this girl's brain, adult regulation of behavior has not yet moved in. That puts her at risk.

In ancient times, and still today, to break from the family might mean death. To tell the truth about families is an extremely difficult and touchy subject. But touch it we must, in the next chapter.

CHAPTER 17

FAMILY AS FRIENDS

"Fate chooses our relatives, we choose our friends."
—Jacques Delille, poet

In the beginning of the book, we said human aloneness drives friendship. We also mentioned three basic traits of friends: they keep us company; they make us feel more relaxed and secure; they make us want the relationship to continue.

But friendship is more than the absence of loneliness. We seek to be a priority in the lives of others. That puts a spring in our step. That's what cuts across all relationship categories, from animals, to friends, to family members, to romantic partners.

In this chapter we consider family as friends because friends and family can exist in a combination which is neither wholly one nor the other.

In 2007, scientists from the University of London reported on their experiment with an "invisible chair."[1] The invisible chair is a standard ski training exercise. It consists of putting your back against a wall while putting your thighs and calves at a right angle to each other. For skiers, it builds strength in the quadriceps; for the rest of us, it is pure torture.

The experiment was designed to determine who holds the highest priority in our lives, and it posed a simple question. How much pain would you put up with for yourself or someone else?

Participants were told for every 20 seconds they could hold the position 70 British pounds would be given to the person of their choice. That person could be themselves, an immediate family member, a best friend, a stranger, someone in their extended family, or a distant family member.

Immediate family includes parents and children, while extended family includes grandparents, aunts, uncles, nieces, nephews, and cousins. Charity was used as a proxy for strangers.

Since participants were denied access to the time, they couldn't objectively tell how long they held the position.

Perhaps it isn't a surprise that people held the position longest for themselves. That was followed, in order, by immediate family, best friends, extended family, and distant kin. Charity (strangers) finished dead last.

There was one noteworthy deviation in the results. The findings were truer of men than of women. This signaled that women act more equitably toward others regardless of the degree of relatedness.

In another experiment, this one in Finland, 30 women watched a film dealing with a moral dilemma.[2] The film was a shortened version of *My Sister's Keeper*, a movie about a sister refusing to donate a kidney to her younger sister.

The catch was half the viewers were told the sisters were biologically related, while half were told the younger sister was adopted as a newborn.

Although 90% of the viewers claimed the biological tie did not matter to them, their brains scans told a different story. Those who believed there was a genetic connection had increased activity in brain areas linked to morals, feelings, and decisions.

As lead researcher Mareike Bacha-Trams said, "The brain sees these two situations very differently."[3]

In the following letter, a mother-in-law demonstrates just how important blood ties are to her.

Family as Friends

I met my husband 10 years ago and at that time had a son, two, from a previous relationship. We married and went on to have three more children.

My husband is a father to my son. My mother-in-law says things aloud to me and my husband about how blood relatives are different and basically if you're not blood you don't matter. If you ask her how many grandkids she has, the number is one less because my son is not counted.

Well, we don't live like this. My son is also my husband's son and a member of this family. I am upset because my mother-in-law sends cards for birthdays to the other three kids and not my son. My husband told her that's not right. She doesn't care.

My husband's brother lost his first marriage because of this family. They blame his wife when I know it was them. They are terrible and have never accepted either my son or me. They talk about their other in-laws badly. I can only imagine what they say about me.

I have tried so hard. I used to call all the time since they live out of town. But they just don't think I am good enough. I don't care. I can deal with my end. I just can't deal with them not acknowledging my son.

My son's birthday is in January, and if they forget again, my plan is to write my mother-in-law a letter and send back all the old cards. How is it that he is the oldest kid and they simply forget? Is sending the cards back the right thing to do? Should I call on the phone?

I am to the point where it is going to be hard to be nice and decent about it. Everyone tells me to tell them to their face, but I am afraid my marriage will suffer. My husband just doesn't have the guts to stand up and deal with confrontation.

-Susan

Susan, on *Sesame Street*, characters often played the game One of These Things. Four objects would be grouped together, like three shoes and a spoon. Then a puppet or person would sing, "One of these things is not like the other, one of these things just doesn't belong."

In a terrible variation on that game, your mother-in-law is trying to teach the younger children that your son doesn't belong in the family. What she is doing is cruel.

Your son is brother to the other three children. The four are being raised together, and your son has existed throughout their existence. Your mother-in-law diminishes and dismisses that relationship. In effect, she is telling the other kids your son is not their brother.

In his book *Monday Morning Choices* David Cottrell makes an unusual statement. "Choose the right enemies." That remark takes people aback, but it's true. Based on the values you hold, some people will be your friend and others your enemy. Accept it.

Treat her in accordance with how she is. Don't think kindness always works. It doesn't. It often reinforces bad behavior, rather than changing it.

Aside from this problem, there is another problem. Your husband has diminished himself in your eyes. He is supposed to be the love of your life and your champion, yet he won't stand up to his mother. If he won't stand up for equality of treatment, you must balance the scales for the well-being of all the children.

The birthday cards are like the wedges used to split logs and your mother-in-law is using them to split your family.

Send the cards back with a note. Tell your mother-in-law she is not allowed to create a rift among your children. Tell her your son is something to her: he is half-brother to the other three children and, in your family, a full-fledged brother and son.

-Wayne & Tamara

The letter above may explain the experience of James Michener.[4] Michener was a foundling who never knew who his parents were. His surname was actually the name of his adoptive mother.

Michener wrote the book behind the musical *South Pacific*, and his novels topped bestseller lists for 40 years.

Family as Friends

Yet when he rose to prominence as a writer, he started receiving anonymous notes like the following. "You don't know who I am but I sure know who you are. You aren't a Michener and never were. You're a fraud to go around using that good name and you ought to be ashamed of yourself." The notes were signed "A real Michener."

The venom reached a frantic level when James Michener won the Pulitzer Prize, with the anonymous writer asking indignantly, "Who in hell do you think you are, trying to be better than you are?"

People's attitude toward family varies. For some people, their family is a source of affection. For others, it is a source of infection.

In his essay on friendship, Michel de Montaigne asks, "Why is it necessary that rapport, which begets true friendship, should always meet in family relations? A father and a son may be of contrary dispositions, and so may brothers: he is my son, he is my brother, but he is hotheaded, churlish, or a fool."[5]

Lydia Denworth put it more simply. "Being related is not a guarantee of affinity."[6]

But when friends feel a strong emotional bond, they may use kin terms like "brother from another mother" or "sister from another mister" to describe their closeness. They feel akin to each other, as if family.

And, of course, some people include family members in their tightest circle of friends.

The following letter poses a moral choice involving blood ties.

My partner and I have been together 10 years. We own our own home, so obviously our credit is joined. Both individually and together we have always had excellent credit; we are never late with a payment and never overextended.

We recently found out my partner's sister fraudulently opened up credit accounts using my partner's name without her knowledge or approval. This sister has racked up $11,000 in debt and is way behind in payments. We *found this out because we were denied credit. Prior to this our credit score was at the top of the chart.*

We notified our local police, filed a report, alerted credit bureaus and other agencies. The police advised us to alert the local police in the state where her sister lives in order to further pursue the identity theft.

Herein lies the problem. Her sister, an adult in her middle 30s with a good-paying job, still resides at home with her parents. Her father is employed with law enforcement in the area and also is considering running for mayor of the town. Both her parents are very active in the local Catholic church.

Out of respect we approached her father before going to the local police. As it turns out, this is not the first time her sister has done this. She has a long history of poor financial decisions and deceptions, including doing almost the same thing to her parents. She is also a pathological liar.

My partner is torn about what to do. If she does not go to the police, this fraudulent information will stay on her credit history for 10 years. If we pursue the identity theft, my partner will be the "bad guy" for turning in her sister. Her father does not want her to pursue this because he wants to protect his daughter from prosecution.

I say her father should be concerned about protecting the daughter who has always done the right thing and to uphold the law, even if it is his own daughter who has done wrong. What do you advise?

-Mallory

Mallory, the motto of many law enforcement agencies is "Protect and serve." Your partner's father wants to protect and serve himself and the perpetrator of a crime, not the victim of the crime and the community at large. He believes it is okay to send someone else's daughter, brother, or sister to jail, but not his own.

The term identity theft makes this crime sound like dressing up for Halloween or using a fake ID to get into a bar, but it amounts to grand theft, embezzlement, robbery, and fraud. Ideally your partner could handle this as a mental health issue and get restitution as well as help for her sister. Practically speaking that isn't going to happen.

Your partner's sister holds all the power and always will, unless something is done. Victimizing her sibling doesn't make the crime less, it makes it worse. A crime against a person we have a bond with adds another level to the betrayal, and adults well into their 30s need to live in accordance with adult rules.

Think about the idea of the "bad guy." This kind of bad guy is bad only to those trying to ladle guilt onto a person who acts responsibly. This kind of bad guy is bad only to those seeking to be immune from the consequences of their actions. This kind of bad guy becomes bad only by allowing herself to become a coconspirator in a cover-up which will harm others at a later date.

Living in accordance with reality, rather than with appearances, simplifies life marvelously. Sometimes in life you have to be the bad guy. If your partner's sister ever gets the mental health help she needs, it's more likely to come from butting against the legal system than from being sheltered from it.

-Wayne and Tamara

A Turkish proverb says, "Better a true friend than a relation."

Barrel of Apples

My older sister and brother cut me off if I don't agree with them. Most of my life, I've known this and kept my mouth shut and my opinions to myself.

Five years ago, my sister cut me off because I told her I only had four days to get together during the holidays. So two years later she sends me a letter expressing how jealous she is of me because I have a good job, happy family, and a nice house. But she has all those things too. I did not respond. It's always something with her, and I'm tired of her head games.

My brother has always been a bachelor, going from one woman to the next. He prefers much younger women. Five years ago, my son went to visit and my brother was mean to him, even cruel. I did not confront him; I just didn't put my son in that position again.

My brother travels abroad. His last girlfriend said he goes to prostitutes and brothels and forwarded emails and photos as proof. Again, I kept my mouth shut.

After he split with her, he decided not to get a place to live. He decided to travel to family members and friends' houses, staying up to two months at a time. I call it his I'm-taking-advantage-of-you tour.

He called a week before Christmas saying he was bringing his latest young girlfriend to my house. I told him no. He got irate and sent me a long email saying I'm a horrible person and he will never talk to me again.

I can live happily not being abused any longer, but because of what happened with my brother, our 79-year-old mother has little to do with me. It's sad. At the same time I'm emotionally exhausted trying to keep peace in this dysfunctional family. Any suggestions?

-Kerry

Kerry, we have one suggestion. Celebrate!

Your sister didn't have anyone to abuse at the moment and she missed abusing you. She was willing to say she was jealous of you even though you know she was not. She should have apologized to you, but you know she never will.

Fortunately, you said no. And your brother? He doesn't belong in your home. Again, you said no.

In the real world, when a victim says no, the abuse continues. In the best of worlds, the victim says no and the abuse stops. In a perfect world, the victim says no and the abusers say, "I'm cutting you off."

You are living in the perfect world.

The only problem is your mother, who plays minion to the other two. Don't change what is right to please her.

-Wayne & Tamara

Kin are defined as those related to us by blood or by marriage.

The following letter is about a blood relative. The second letter involves kin by marriage. The question is, what is there of friendship in either letter?

I just read an email from a close cousin. She said, "What you did was too harsh." She was referring to me leaving my husband, a close friend of her family.

I don't know how to respond, but I'm thinking how do people decide when someone's hurt enough to do something about it? How do we measure pain when it's not ours?

After a year and a half I left. He was shocked. I hugged him, kissed him, held his hand and told him to take good care of himself, then got on a plane back home to the place I left.

I didn't leave for another man. Our marriage was strained from the outset, and we couldn't seem to get a grip. He's angry; he doesn't think he hurt me "enough to warrant leaving."

He cried when I left; those who saw this are sorry for this man who has been "abandoned." These are the same people I begged for a year and a half to intervene and help us find a way.

I don't know if I should scream or go under a rock.

-Claudia

Claudia, you can admire someone who tries to intervene when they see another in pain, but your cousin is reacting to his pain, not yours. Your cousin's solution for his pain is to put you in pain.

When kids are playing and wrestle or fight, they understand they must respect the word "uncle." When one says, "Uncle," the other one is supposed to stop.

There has always been that give-way word. In The Game of Thrones the expression is "I yield." In the military it's the white flag.

You said uncle. You did the hard thing, packed up and left. That has to be respected. You don't have to be hurt enough that you hate him. You don't have to allow him to hurt you more before uncle is respected.

Mistakes get made. People marry the wrong person.

It doesn't matter what your cousin's motives are. She can feel as she feels. You don't have to respond.

-Wayne & Tamara

Big Bad Wolf

I have been friends with my sister-in-law for 25 years. I've been there for her during many heartbreaking situations, even putting my marriage on the line at times.

Our relationship has been mostly one-sided. My sister-in-law is self-centered, demanding, and doesn't hold back on being deliberately cruel if things don't go her way. Due to my forgiving nature and dislike of confrontation, I tried to rise above it all.

That is, until now. I am going through an extremely unpleasant divorce. My ex moved on and said and did damaging things. Still I keep it all bottled up inside and never say a bad word against him to his family.

My brother-in-law recently confided that under the pretense of a nice day out, my sister- and mother-in-law plan to pump me for information to pass along to my ex. My brother-in-law says he is disgusted with what they are saying and wants me to know what I am up against.

Comments he passed on make me know he's telling the truth. I am appalled. My in-laws always said I'm the most wonderful person with the loveliest disposition of anyone they ever met. I thought they genuinely cared about me.

Obviously, I do not want to engage in any way with my sister-in-law, but she's pushing to meet with me. I wish to call it a day, in writing, as I will be a wreck if I have to do it verbally. How can I do this without betraying my brother-in-law's confidence?

-Simone

Simone, there are two reasons not to put your feelings in writing. One, it makes you appear weak, and two, it gives your in-laws something concrete to criticize, and they will nitpick every statement and comma in your letter.

Like the first of the Three Little Pigs, you've been living in a house of straw. It is easy to describe your disposition as motivated by kindness, but in fact it is motivated by fear. You think writing a letter is like building a house of sticks, but the true solution is to build a house of bricks.

Your sister-in-law and her mother didn't tell you what their game plan is. You don't need to tell them your game plan or what you know. At your door or on the phone all you need is a simple, curt refusal. If you must use an excuse, tell them the upheaval of the divorce makes you unwilling to get together.

Your new life is beginning; you are going to be master of your world. In small steps and safe situations put your needs first. Utter your opinions, beliefs, and feelings without apology. Slowly expand your comfort zone. The more you practice this, the easier it will get.

Your sister- and mother-in-law can huff and puff all they want, but they are not entitled to take advantage of you. No, they aren't. Not by the hair on your chinny-chin-chin.

-Wayne & Tamara

From an evolutionary point of view, why do we have friends?

The obvious answer is there are so many dimensions to our lives that relatives can't possibly fill all the roles.[8] There simply aren't enough kin to go around to meet our needs. In addition, some things are so personal or intimate we might not want to share them with a blood relative.

We only have two hands. Kin give us more hands, but friends vastly extend our reach. What to wear, what to pack, where to go, how to behave, who to call. Those are only a few things friends can help us with.

Moreover, brothers and sisters have their own social networks. And parents? Well, they typically act like parents. But friends are our psychological equals and peers, even if they are younger or older.

That doesn't mean we can trust all our would-be friends. Many people do not qualify. Boncompagno of Signa, a 13th century Italian writer, listed 29 different kinds of friends, nearly all of them bad.[9] He gave them names like fair-weather friend, counterfeit friend, turncoat friend, and mercenary friend.

One difference between family and close friends is often this. We help family simply because they are family. We help friends because we feel like it. If we are fortunate, some members of our family feel like a best friend.

There is still one category of friends we haven't dealt with: romantic friends. They deserve a chapter all to themselves.

CHAPTER 18
ROMANTIC FRIENDS

"Friendship is constant in all other things, Save in the office and affairs of love."

—Shakespeare

Our need for love and sex can be one of the strongest challenges to friendship because it puts two strong drives in competition.

A year ago, I was having a difficult time and slowly rebuilding my life when I met the most wondrous girl in the world. Until three months ago our relationship was perfect. Then bad things occurred.

We ended up on opposite shifts and I rarely saw her because I worked nights. I asked my friend Larry to make sure she got out of the house and look after her. I thought everything was fine until three weeks ago when we broke up.

The night after we broke up, Larry took me out to drown my sorrows. He bought me drinks, told me she cheated, and egged me on. Then he said she was coming to the bar. Needless to say, when she arrived sparks flew. It wasn't a pretty sight. Larry said he would patch things up. Every day, he said, he was working on getting her back for me.

Three days ago, I found out Larry worked for six months to tarnish my reputation in her eyes. Now he is wining and dining my girlfriend and showering her with flowers.

Yesterday, I accidentally ran into my girlfriend. We talked, and now she knows Larry lied to both of us. She wants me to leave her alone for a while; then she will call. But Larry sent me an email saying they are now an official couple and very much in love.

I would dearly love to patch things up with her. But now I'm lost as to what to do.

-Jeremy

An unusual word has made it into the Urban Dictionary, though it isn't mainstream yet.[1] The word is "cucklord." A cucklord is defined as a man who actively discredits other men to get to a woman he covets. That describes Larry.

Rick Springfield popularized the song "Jessie's Girl" about a man who wants his friend's girlfriend. That desire is found in both genders.

I have a friend I've known since high school. We had a habit of hanging out and then not talking to each other for months on end. But when we do talk, it's like we've talked every day.

Anyway, she had a boyfriend and they were in a casual relationship. He was interested in me and she was cool with that. Now, months later, I'm crashing at their place. Now she's no longer cool with it.

Recently they fought and broke up. She asked me not to sleep with him, but I've developed feelings for him. I've never felt this way about anyone. I'm 23 and have never gotten past the "You're cute, let's date" point in a relationship.

It's different with him. He's all I can think about and he makes me feel special and wanted. I have no idea if it would be just sex for him, but the things he says and does make me think he likes me for more.

I'm super awkward and don't even know where to begin. I don't want to hurt my friend, but I owe it to myself to see where things go. I saw him today and things got a bit handsy.

I know someone's going to end up getting hurt, and mostly I don't want that person to be me. What do I do?

-Harper

Harper, you've decided you are going for him regardless of what your friend thinks. Okay, but it's not nice to eat fries off someone else's plate without permission.

Tell your friend what you told us.

-Wayne & Tamara

Often the person left out is not a rival but a same-sex friend.

It sounds silly, but I feel so down today. My best friend, Erica, has a new boyfriend, and they are completely wrapped up in each other. It's not just this. Not only do I feel left out, as I haven't got a boyfriend myself, but I know she has told him some things about me. He must have a really bad impression of me.

It is hard trying to be nice to her when we go out together. All through the evening it is blatantly obvious all she's doing is thinking of him. It's like I don't matter anymore. Erica said she was going on holiday with me and another friend, but I learned she is about to cancel. She told her boyfriend I would probably get in a stress and not talk to her for a week.

I am really annoyed, but I don't want to be pathetic. This is the main problem, but I also worry about my weight. Men don't find me attractive. I long to do something about it, but I don't have the willpower. I start a diet then resort to eating lots of chocolate and crisps. If you could tell me what to do, I would appreciate it so much.

-Sandra

Sandra, Erica is wrapped up in a new boyfriend. Give her the chance to be with him and explore their newness. In time some of the shine will wear off. It is no different than if her mother were ill or she started a new job.

She has added claims on her time, but in time your friendship will regain its equilibrium.

Sometimes we don't understand the meaning of events in our lives. As someone once said, "How we view the problem is the problem." Erica's new adventure has put you at a crossroads. You have been given an opportunity to add new friends and other things which will enhance your life. Use this time to boost yourself up and focus on what you need to do.

You are in conflict between who you are and who you want to be. Between wanting to be thin and wanting to eat chocolate. Every day you want to change, and every day you fail. You are of two minds, and being of two minds makes stress inevitable. Either accept yourself as you are or figure out the way to change.

-Wayne & Tamara

A common problem with both genders is learning to accept no.

I'm a girl, 17, and I have known this guy my whole life. The boy I'm talking about is dealing with a lot right now. Four months ago, his mom was diagnosed with breast cancer and recently started treatment.

We were church friends until last summer when we worked at camp together. As you can guess, I developed feelings for him. We suspected it would happen, but I never made my feelings clear because he told me he didn't want that and I didn't want to get hurt.

The more I kept it a secret the more hurt I got, especially since one of my best friends was becoming close to him.

I was so stressed, after five months I told him the truth. He told me he knew. I was hurt he didn't confront me about it because I thought we had more trust than that.

He doesn't believe this is a big deal and doesn't appreciate that I put him in this position because he already made it clear he doesn't like me that way. I was so hurt and confused I didn't attend church for two months.

Recently I started going back, and he's noticed I don't look him in the eye. Since my return, we've had numerous texting conversations. In the first I apologized for everything. The rest were to see how he was or him texting me stupid questions. "Who did you sit with at the hockey game?" "Are you having people over this weekend?"

Once, after I yet again apologized, he freaked out and said he was tired of me making him feel guilty and trying to change his feelings.

But I'm still hurt he doesn't like me, isn't too concerned about being friends again, and is so close with my best friend. I'm trying desperately to fix this and he doesn't even care.

Now, I don't want to make him out to be a bad guy; after all he's got a lot on his plate right now, even if that's no excuse.

You may say I need to let it all go. And in most cases you'd be right, but this is someone I have to see once or twice a week. We have a lot of friends in common. I can't just shut him out or act like it's no big deal.

I can tell whenever it's brought up, it causes him grief, and he doesn't want to discuss it further. How do I fix this?

-Hanna

Hanna, a few days ago, Tamara showed me a YouTube video of horses clustered on a grassy hilltop in the mountains.

A mountain biker, a grown man, brazenly moves toward one horse, who seems to be standing guard over the others. This horse doesn't care for the man's advance. As the man draws nearer, it swishes its tail back and forth. Yet the man doesn't break stride, even when the horse puts its ears flat against its head.

As the horse goes stiff-legged, its entire body rigid, the man walks closer and holds out his hand to touch the horse's muzzle. In a flash the horse bites the man's arm, breaking the flesh but not the bone. The man retreats in pain.

Three times the horse signaled Do Not Advance. Three times the man ignored him. Does this situation sound familiar?

This boy wants you as a friend. He thinks despite your feelings, you will stop coming on to him. He wants things to be the way they should be once someone tells another no.

And somehow you think he is the inconsiderate one.

A bad guy would trifle with you and take advantage of your crush. Be glad he isn't that kind of guy.

Be patient. Someday you'll find a man who shares your feelings, a man who won't put his ears back at your advance.

-Wayne

For 30 years, psychologists claimed that men exaggerate women's sexual interest in them.[2] Lately there's been an about-face on that idea. Some researchers suggest that women minimize their own level of interest in a man.[3]

Researchers Carin Perilloux and Robert Kurzban summed up this view when they said, "Men appear to overestimate women's sexual intentions [only] because women understate them."

In spite of this, some women and some men will not accept that their interest is not reciprocated.

I am going nuts, which is why I am writing.

I have been "dating" a man for a year now. I say "dating" because we are platonic, and he is having trouble rebounding from a marriage that dissolved three years ago. I should have moved on and would have if we hadn't connected so deeply. He is me in so many ways and complements me in so many others.

For someone like me who scoffed at love, I now crave that very thing from this man. I try to move on, but he is there. We spend hours talking. We have similar educational backgrounds and intellectual pursuits. We enjoy the same jokes and movies.

So much compatibility, yet he wants me to move on. I don't want to go and I don't want to stay. Is this all I can hope for? I've waited all of my 32 years to meet what I consider a soul mate.

Is there anything I can do just to make him release that pain and move on? Even if he chooses someone else, I care too deeply for him to live trapped in "what if" and "what could I have done differently."

Conversely, I don't want to stay and have him shatter my heart. He told me he is not the one for me. But I am assuming by what he says he is not the one for anyone because he failed with this woman he loved.

He also stated he didn't want to introduce sex into our relationship because it would ruin it. I don't want just sex from him. I am hoping for a meaningful relationship that leads to marriage.

-Gloria

Gloria, you've got a great best friend. He is a wonderful part of your life. Unfortunately, your friend is a man. Since he's male, you are trying to turn him into something he is not.

If your heart gets broken, it will be a self-inflicted wound. Your friend has made clear what his role in your life is. If you accept it, you will have a friend who makes the good times merrier and the sad times less sad.

There are those who promise to tell you how to win a man's heart. It's as if they are talking about buying a bicycle, with some assembly required. Get a pair of pliers and perform a few simple tasks and you will have a bicycle you can ride.

A list of compatible qualities, unlike bicycle parts, cannot be put together to make what you want. A husband. Your friend is not an object you can project your will onto.

-Wayne & Tamara

Many men and women share a basic friendship interest in each other. Often the romantic part is no more than familiarity.

My dilemma starts four years ago when my girlfriend of five years broke up with me. It was a rough time. I was just reaching 30 and had recently purchased an engagement ring. I took it hard but fell into my music and in a few months I was back on my feet again.

My ex-girlfriend and I have had ups and downs in other relationships since we broke up but have managed to stay close friends. People think this is strange, since the breakup was not a pleasant one.

Recently she acknowledged feelings of regret about dumping me and said wonderful things that helped subdue feelings of resentment I had toward her. Even so, it was obvious she was just lonely and didn't have anyone in her life at the time.

A few weeks went by and like a fool I slept with her. The passion that had once been was not there, and it felt like we were just going through the motions. I went back on the road to produce a show, and while I was gone, my mind started to relive the love and feelings I once had for her.

But when I returned, she was cold to me. She met someone new, and once again I was in second place. Yesterday, I finally realized I had fallen under the same spell she had. There was no one in my life and I used her to fill the void.

-Corey

The pattern is simply: one of them gets lonely ... the relationship gets physical ... the loneliness abates ... yet something is still missing. When two friends come together like this, they may cure their loneliness, but they still yearn for more.

Corey and his ex are friends, not lovers. The rest of it isn't there.

The problem in the following letter couldn't be more obvious, but the writer doesn't see it.

I have known this woman a bit over a year. At that time she was getting divorced from a damaging marriage. We met at a mutual friend's birthday celebration and really hit it off. We started hanging out, going for drinks, dinner, and movies. I knew almost from day one I was interested and that interest turned into caring.

That scared me quite a bit because of previous times I started having feelings for somebody too quickly. Eventually I let my feelings slip to one of her friends I believed I could trust, and it got back to her. Almost all correspondence stopped. I would call to see how she was doing, and she would not return any of my calls.

Finally, after a month of not hearing from her, she would call out of the blue and say we needed to do something together soon, but the plans always fell through. And so it went for months. I later found out part of the reason she wouldn't call back was because of whatever boyfriend she was seeing at the time.

As time went on we started hanging out again, having great conversations, and exchanging playful glances. Finally I got up the guts to talk to her about all the signals I thought she was giving me. We decided to go get some dinner and see a movie.

That evening, she brought a friend she had not seen in a long time. They were flirting the entire time at dinner and started making out in front of me at the movie. Needless to say I was shocked and utterly heartbroken. A few nights later, I talked to her. She said she didn't feel the same way about me but needed my friendship.

So we left it at that for a while.

However, our relationship has evolved over time. I've seen her through several boyfriends and always been there for her to count on. Sometimes we hang out till the early morning hours talking about everything.

In my own attempt to analyze the situation, I came to the realization the reason we didn't get together was fear: her fear of losing me in a relationship and my fear of her rejecting my affections.

Once a mutual friend of ours told me she saw this woman doing things to get my attention and giving me looks usually reserved for those in love. So here

I am wondering if she really loves me. I have no idea what to think or do about this situation.

-Ed

Ed, there is an interesting short film on visual perception. In the film, six people pass around two basketballs. Half the people wear white shirts and half wear black shirts. As they pass the balls, the players move in a weave pattern. Viewers are asked to count the total number of times the balls are passed.

What viewers are not told is that a person in a gorilla suit will walk into the middle of the basketball players, turn and face the camera, then walk away in the other direction. More than half the people who view this film never see the gorilla. This phenomenon is called inattention blindness, and it refers to the fact we often cannot see what we don't expect to see.

In your case, you cannot see what you don't want to see. A woman brought another man to your dinner and movie date with her. That was the clearest possible way to inform you that you are not in her dating circle. That is the way it has always been for her.

The reasons you think you will one day be together are like the basketball players. They keep you from seeing the gorilla. When a woman treats a man like a confidante and girlfriend, it means she is not interested in that man as a man.

-Wayne & Tamara

Crushes are not just for teenagers, and often they reflect no more than a basic need.

Teacher's Pet
I am 32 and a mom with two children. I've pretty much been single for two years. My problem is I found myself falling for my son's teacher. I never saw a

ring on his finger, so last school year I made every attempt to visit my son's school as often as I could.

Eventually I took the chicken's way out and emailed this man and told him how I felt. He replied that he was flattered, we can remain friends, and he is my child's teacher. I emailed back saying I didn't know what I was doing and was not sure how uncomfortable things would be. He said it would be fine, no feelings hurt.

Once again he is teaching my child, and I still feel the same way. He is such a great man, so dedicated to the kids in his class. He is the man I want to get to know better. I have only seen him once this school year, but we often talk on the phone, though always about my son.

We get along so well and laugh like it is natural. Whether he is just being nice I don't know. After this year he will no longer be my child's teacher. Is there any way for me to find out if he'd like to continue talking? I'm hoping for more. I've been hurt in the past, but with him it just feels so different, so right.

-Anya

Anya, if you expect to have the right to say no and you want that listened to and respected, then you have to know he has the same right. He said no. When you get a no, you move on.

If your lottery ticket is one number off, it doesn't matter. As much as you would like it to be a winner, the numbers don't match and you don't have the winning ticket. There is no sense dwelling on it. Badgering him will make it less likely he will want to talk with you at all.

There is one great positive in this. You have come in contact with a good man with the characteristics you've been looking for. He has given you a model for what you want. You want a man who makes you feel like this one.

This teacher is teaching you a lesson. He has been patient with you. Show him that you have learned. As Thomas Carruthers said, "A teacher is one who makes himself progressively unnecessary."

-Wayne & Tamara

In opposite-sex friendships, sometimes one party feels the two share a common romantic interest. To hold that illusion, they imagine the other person is using reverse psychology on them, though the other person is simply not interested.

I need an outsider's perspective because I can't ask my close friends. I am 21 and one of my best friends is 26. I met him a year ago through a mutual friend, and upon our first meeting we talked all night about life and such. Ever since then I've harbored feelings for him.

We didn't become close until this past spring at a party. I was so shy that if it weren't for my sorority sister, I wouldn't have gone at all. Since then we have literally been inseparable.

This past summer he invited me to accompany him to his brother's birthday party. On the way home he brought up the subject of how he couldn't date me. I was totally caught off guard. Who brings up things that aren't on their mind already? And mind you, when you already have this little crush forming, it's hard to bounce back after they tell you.

He then brings up my other sorority sister and wants to know what I think of her, saying, "I wouldn't date her if you don't like her." Well, then they started dating, and everybody loves them together. They're so cute together and so forth.

Which is why I can't bring this up to my closest friends. I don't want to destroy the golden couple because, believe it or not, I was on the opposite side once and a "sister" swooped in and took my guy away from me.

My best friend and I are still inseparable. We talk for hours a week. I don't think I've ever felt this way about anyone—guy or girlfriend. With him I can be myself. He understands my sense of humor and knows what I'm going to say before I say it.

But it's getting harder to see them together. She now considers me one of her closest friends too and is so happy I played a mild part in putting them together.

Romantic Friends

So here are my choices: continue to be their closest friend and never tell him; tell him how I feel and risk losing one of the closest friendships I've had in years; or slowly distance myself from them, which is hard to do because we spend so much time together.

-Nikki

Nikki, do you need him to tell you again he doesn't find you attractive in that way? What would that do to your friendship? And your morale?

The added little something that changes a great friend into the one for you isn't there. Asking about it will strain him. Things will get more awkward. He doesn't need to give you a no.

Because he brought the issue up, you would like to believe he was thinking about dating you. It is more likely he knows you would like to date him and he gave you his answer.

Don't exactly separate yourself from the "golden couple," but have more time apart so your one can appear. Perhaps the kismet here is through him you will meet the man for you or the space you create between you and him will allow the right one to appear.

Part of why you covet him is that he is all you see. But your relationship is not "eyes across a crowded room and some enchanted evening." Don't be stuck hoping he will warm up to you like a comfortable old robe.

The unsaid core of the relationship self-help industry is these books are not about changing yourself; they are about helping yourself to someone else. That doesn't work.

Care about him as a friend, want the best for him. If he is happy with her, that should make you happy too. But free yourself to find what your heart desires.

-Wayne & Tamara

Occasionally the friends-to-lovers scenario is actually true, though when it happens, it happens in its own time.

I have a male friend with whom I share everything except physical interaction. In 15 years there has been no sex, no kissing, no intimacies. We share a rare and true platonic love.

We talk about everything, including sex, ex-lovers, money, religion, politics, needs, wants, and hurtful experiences. Or we sit and work on a project for hours without talking at all. We laugh at ourselves and each other and both think the other is strong and intelligent.

This friendship was uncomfortable for our spouses when we were married, but it did not play a part in either divorce. We are known and accepted by all family members, including children from our previous marriages. However, some of our friends and family do not like to be around us because, "Everyone else is invisible when you two are together."

We often email each other at the same time, or he will page me when I am thinking of him. It is permissible within our relationship to sign paperwork for each other, such as charging tickets or approving carpentry work. He is renovating a house and consults me on everything from wall color to wall placement.

Now, please don't think it is all rainbows and lollipops. We disagree (rarely, but it happens). We aggravate each other, but when getting on each other's nerves, we say so. Neither of us is involved with anyone else, and neither of us is looking.

This has been the way of our relationship for 15 years. Now, in the past two months, there has been a reserve between us that was never there before. It is something we have not spoken about. We now go to great lengths to avoid touching, even accidentally. Six months ago, an accidental bump would have gone unnoticed. Now it brings mutterings of apology and careful body placements.

I have never seen him totally naked but thought nothing of him answering the door in a towel fresh from the shower. I'd barge right in, make some coffee, and comment he better start eating, he was losing too much weight. Now I'd still barge in and make coffee, but I would not have the composure to maintain inane chatter. In 15 years, I doubt he noticed that I have breasts, but he did the other day.

Which brings us to the problem. The relationship is still intact, but there is an added dimension I cannot grasp. Surely at our age, late forties, it is not some post-adolescent sexual awareness. Is it possible, or advisable, for platonic friends to add a physical dimension to their relationship?

-Marla

Marla, usually when a man and a woman are friends it's because one or both don't see the other as someone they would date. Then, after being friends, one party decides to turn the friendship into an intimate relationship. When they write us, the question is, "How can I do this?"

Our initial thought is they want to know how to approach the other person. As we continue reading, we learn they have already asked and been rebuffed. You can hear the desperation in the letter. Nearly always they claim they don't want to ruin the friendship, but that is exactly what they are doing.

None of those red flags are in your letter. What is missing in those letters is a sense of connection, the sort of connection your friends and family see. We scoured your letter for negatives. We looked for contradictions, mixed messages, and hidden agendas. We can't find any.

Who knows why the door was closed for so long? Maybe neither of you was ready. Love doesn't come on command. It comes when it comes. For whatever reason, it seems the door has now opened. We are not fortune tellers. We cannot tell you what will happen, but when a door opens for you, you walk in.

-Wayne & Tamara

Some research about friends-with-benefits suggests that people in these relationships are not lovers. They are no closer than friends.

A young man wrote about his girlfriend:

My partner and I were together 10 months. When we got together, she had just broken up from a three-year relationship. She started with me soon after and never took the time to heal and find closure. We just took to each other and ran.

We had our ups and downs, and I guess because she struggled with a lot and tried to make me happy, I fell in love with her. We spoke about a baby and getting married. We were so good together. Now she is telling me she cannot be in a relationship because we did it all wrong.

She says she needs to do what she needs to do because she cannot give me 100 percent. She is a missionary and travels to Africa a lot. She doesn't say when she is okay, we can start over. She says we do not know what the future holds...

We told this young man, if she loved him, things would be right for her. We said, "Why is she picking it apart? Because this cake doesn't taste right. Was there salt in the sugar? Bugs in the flour? A forgotten ingredient? Yes, that's it. A forgotten ingredient. Love."

Working Girl
I am falling hard for my best guy friend. We have a friends-with-benefits relationship. He also pays for things for me and cooks for me. He even stated he wants to take me to Japan next year, which is my dream vacation. I am basically part of his family.

He says one thing he wants is a family and to find a girl who does also. Well, that's me! The problem? He still loves his ex and he told me he isn't attracted to me. I think otherwise. Should I talk to him about it or keep our relationship the same and hope he sees me as more than one of his best friends?
-Tatyana

Tatyana, he talks to you about the woman he hopes to marry, and he's decided that isn't you. Staying with him as a friend-with-benefits may get you a trip to Japan, but you may never be more than his geisha.

-Wayne & Tamara

The problem with talking about friends-with-benefits is that the term itself is ambiguous. Some researchers claim it can be divided into as many as seven distinct situations, largely because the expectations of each partner are different.[4]

Are we talking about sex with no strings attached or are we talking about a romantic recipe—take a cup of friendship, add sex, stir, see what happens? Or perhaps we are talking about something else.

One study suggests that only about 15% of the time do friends-with-benefits transition into a romantic relationship, even though that is what one of the partners desires.[5]

The poet Arthur Symons wrote, "I cannot, having been your lover, Stoop to become your friend!" In our experience, this is often true because one of the partners still wants more.

Taken for a Ride

I suppose I am writing because I need advice… more advice than my friends have offered … or better advice than my friends have offered.

Sometime in late November I ran into an acquaintance on campus and he offered me a ride home from class. Instead we went for lunch and by the end of lunch he asked me out to a movie and dinner that night.

We got to know each other very quickly, and although it was out of the blue, I quickly learned that I enjoyed his company tremendously. We spent all our time together for the following two weeks.

I hate to sound cliché and say we just clicked, but the truth is, we did. I've never clicked with anyone that quickly, and I've had my share of boyfriends. We quickly became romantic and were seemingly very into each other.

After two weeks something changed in his attitude toward me and I confronted him. We had a very open talk about how we both became comfortable with each other very quickly. He confessed he had just broken up with someone and was not completely over her.

We decided we would start over, be friends, and see if it took us back to each other. He seemed genuine when he said he still wanted to hang out. I was upset about everything but I figured we still had a chance. I have only seen or heard from him once since, on his birthday, when I dropped off a card.

It has been three weeks. I was upset initially but lately feel I've gotten over him. At this point I just want to be friends, perhaps with the hope maybe something will rekindle. I miss his company.

Should I go out on a limb and call him before school starts? Is there any way I can get him back in my life in any way?

-Ashley

Ashley, you thought you clicked. The click you thought you heard was like finding the other shoe of a pair. But was it really that?

You didn't know him. You talked about everything but he didn't tell you about the girlfriend he just broke up with. In a breakup, when you don't really know the other person, you are not likely to get an honest explanation as to why. Often what is said by the one breaking away is said simply so they can break away.

What story have you told us? The story of Cinderella, with a twist. The prince slipped the shoe on my foot and it was a perfect fit. After a couple of weeks he pulled it off and went looking for another Cinderella.

After two magical weeks Prince Charming would not pull the slipper off Cinderella's foot. The magic was mostly on your end. After a one-night stand or a two-week whirlwind romance, when a guy says, "Let's be friends," the relationship is over.

Things happened too quickly with a man you didn't really know, though you are reluctant to admit you didn't really know him. Why? Because "I might not have done what I did had I known more."

When a guy walks away from you, you have to be strong enough to walk away from him. Cinderella didn't chase Prince Charming around saying, "Try it on again! Try it on again!" That's what the mean stepsisters did.

-Wayne & Tamara

In 1997, Art and Elaine Aron and three others published results of an experiment which became famous as 36 Questions.[6] The essence of the experiment was this. Two people sit down and ask each other questions from a list. They begin with innocuous questions like, "Who would you want as a dinner guest if you could choose anyone in the world?"

Then the conversation moves to treasured memories, embarrassing moments, and regrets if you were to die tonight. The pair advise each other on personal problems and exchange compliments—in fact, they exchange compliments five different times, taking turns.

The purpose of the experiment was to generate closeness in an experimental setting. But the questions are often presented as "36 questions that lead to love."

But does the experiment produce real intimacy?

The researchers answered yes and no. Yes, because it mimics what occurs naturally over time, and no, because "it seems unlikely that the procedure produces loyalty, dependence, commitment, or other relationship aspects that might take longer to develop."

That's what Ashley experienced. She gained a quick familiarity with a man, which mostly reflected her own state of mind.

We have often heard married people call their partner their best friend, even though it is obvious they can barely tolerate each other. As a result, we are wary when we hear couples use that term.

But for some couples it is true.

The writer Erica Jong was not a great fan of marriage. But in *Fear of Flying* she said, "Coupling doesn't always have to do with sex."[7] Often, she says, it's "two people depending on each other and babying each other and defending each other against the world outside." For her, she said, it could be worth being married just to have "one friend in an indifferent world."

When some couples part, it appears they were never more than friends.

I am recently separated from my husband of 10 years. He left me for a woman he worked with, and she is currently out of the country. They carry on a long-distance romance. In the meantime, I have gone on with my life and am happy with my new independence.

My husband and I remain friends. In fact, Ron often calls to talk about his new love, and I help out with whatever problems they're having. Unfortunately, he also talks about their sex life to me! This is something I am not comfortable hearing.

I don't want to say this to him because he would take it to mean I still pine for him. I would rather die than have him think that! What can I do to get him to stop telling me what goes on between the sheets?

-Elaine

Elaine, the old saying is "Gentlemen never tell." Since Ron is no gentleman, you must be more direct. Next time he is in the middle of describing things in the bedroom, interrupt him and say, "Ron, TMI. Too much information."

-Wayne & Tamara

The underlying truth in Elaine's marriage is that she and Ron were friends. Though they added a sexual component, they were never more than friends, and in Ron's mind, that's still what they are.

A proverb claims we cannot understand another until we walk a mile in their shoes. A friend, a good friend, must be able to put themselves in our shoes. What would be even better would be if they could put themselves into our body. That is the subject of the next chapter.

CHAPTER 19
THE POWER OF FRIENDS

Between Friends All Is Common.
—Erasmus of Rotterdam

"As a child, I liked to imagine what it would be like to one day wake up in someone else's body," says Pawel Tacikowski, a Swedish neuroscientist. "I guess I've never grown out of it—I just turned it into my job."[1]

Tacikowski and his colleagues at the Karolinska Institutet had pairs of friends rate each other on 120 different qualities while sitting at a computer.[2] The qualities included things such as likeability, talent, bossiness, independence, shyness, cheerfulness, and open-mindedness.

That was the mundane part of the experiment. Then the experimenters did something unusual. They had pairs of friends lie down on adjacent beds and equipped them with head-mounted displays showing a live feed of the other person's body.

The friends were touched in the same place at the same time while they saw their friend's body being touched. After a few minutes, most people felt they had swapped bodies. One participant even told his friend to "Stop moving my toes!"[3]

To make sure the swap was working, each person saw the friend's body being menaced with a mock knife. When that happened, they broke out in a sweat.

While the swap was in progress, the friends were asked to rate themselves on qualities they had previously rated their friend.

What happened was, while "in" the friend's body, their self-image went a bit haywire. Their beliefs about their own personality became similar to their beliefs about their friend. Evidently this occurred so they could maintain a unified sense of self.

The investigators were interested in certain kinds of mental illness, but we wonder what this experiment says about how friends influence each other. We also wonder how much our friends are part of our own sense of self. That is barely explored territory.

When Kevin Ochsner, a cognitive neuroscientist at Columbia University, commented on one brain scan experiment, he said it seemed to pick up traces of "an ineffable shared reality" between friends.[4] We find that line memorable. Neuroscientists don't normally talk like theologians or flower children.

Experiments like the body-swap suggest how friendship, and by extension our entire social network, influences us. But up to now that tale has been told mostly in terms of the anterior cingulate cortex, the hippocampus, and other parts of the brain most of us can't locate.

Jaana Juvonen, a developmental psychologist at UCLA, has done research in a more down-to-earth way.[5] She observes middle school children.

Juvonen found that while teachers often separate friends to reduce the amount of chatter, children work better with friends. "Their dialogue is much deeper, cognitively more complex, than when we ask kids to work with just any classmate."

The same is true of adult friends. A survey by investigators at Ohio State University compared work teams of friends with work teams composed of non-friends or acquaintances.[6] The study involved 1016 teams.

The results were clear. Friendship groups outperformed the other groups. The larger the team the greater the advantage. This advantage held whether the task involved brawn or brains, and the advantage was found in all age groups.

As study coauthor Robert Lount explained, "Working with friends is not just something that makes us feel good—it can actually produce better results."[7] Coauthor Seunghoo Chung explained that friends "know each other's strengths and weaknesses and can figure out how to break up the work in the most efficient way."

Another workplace study specifically focused on "multiplex relationships."[8]

A multiplex relationship is a relationship with more than one context. For example, imagine a doctor with a patient who is a businessman. Sometimes the two play golf together. Sometimes the doctor calls the businessman for financial advice.

These two have three different connections—patient, golf partner, and financial advisor—making the relationship multiplex.

Multiplex relationships are powerful. As an insurance man once told us, if you have to call a doctor "Doctor," you have little chance of making the sale. But if you are on friendly terms and call him or her Frank or Elise, your chances of a sale soar.

In the multiplex study, researchers at Rutgers University asked employees at a company to name people they went to for assistance with job problems. They were also asked to name coworkers they thought of as friends.

What the investigators found is that multiplex relationships increase employee performance.

They attributed this to several things.[9] If you have a friend in the company, it's less daunting to ask them for help than to ask a supervisor, plus friends in other departments can share information you might not otherwise hear. Finally, having work friends keeps people in a better mood, which increases performance.

But there can be a dark side to multiplex relationships. Friendship can be weaponized to make other people suffer.

Recently Ted, a nice coworker, joined my group. We work together on all projects and share ideas and communication with our manager on a daily basis.

Ted started carpooling with the boss. At that point he changed. What were joint projects Ted made his own. When I tried to contact our boss to do the same, it was obvious he prefers Ted. The two of them talk at home and go to church together.

I have been in my group for over two years and work hard to be creative. Now I find anytime I do something, Ted quickly takes over. He always beats me to the punch. I am not trying to be petty, but it is getting ridiculous. A job I have been striving for is finally open. There is a trickled rumor the boss has nominated Ted.

Let me review the facts. I have been here longer, worked harder, and am overdue for promotion, a thought shared by coworkers. I mentioned this to a higher-level boss, who in turn looked at me as a troublemaker.

Direct contact with Ted would be dynamite because of his attitude, but this isn't right. The more waves I make the more I look bad, so I am hoping to get some advice on possible strategy.

-Donald

The letter writer, Donald, has one connection to his boss, as an employee. Ted has three or four—employee, carpooler, social friend, church.

Perhaps Ted and his boss were naturally drawn together. Perhaps, and this is what we suspect, Ted is a shrewd apple-polisher who knows how to use friendship to gain advancement. In that case, Donald can kiss his promotion goodbye.

A final way third parties can suffer in the workplace occurs when friends form a clique.

My boss would like me to write a letter of complaint on what goes on when he is away from the office and I am left alone with two younger coworkers.

When they arrive at the office and clock in, they eat their breakfast in the break room, go on the computer and do personal things, like plan vacations, pay bills and read personal email. Sometimes they nap or leave the office for personal errands. At lunchtime we clock out for 30 minutes, but they continue their lunch break after they clock back in.

They are best friends and hang out together. We all do the same work, and even though they see me working they continue to text, talk about their love life, and plan what to do after hours.

By the time they decide to work, half the day is gone. One will work while the other stands there and continues to gossip, text, or listen to iTunes. When they don't want me to listen to their conversation, they speak in Spanish, a language I don't speak. Next day, when the boss arrives, he wants to know what we each did because so little was accomplished.

I started this job a few months ago and they have been here over a year. They work on the days the boss is in. It's the day he is out of the office that they abuse the system. My boss told me he wants me to write up these women in a report and they will not be fired.

But they will know who complained about them. I'm afraid of retaliation. I want to keep this job. I feel the boss should know what is going on but not use me. How can I write a report against them without them knowing I did it?

-Lizzie

Lizzie, we all have an internal gauge, that no one gave us, which says this is fair and this is not fair. Fairness is valued in business and in life. When it is not met, everyone with a sense of justice notices. "It's not fair." That's where our head goes.

You weren't hired to make these two do their job. They have been there longer and you are not their supervisor. You come to work to do your job and get a paycheck. But for some reason, perhaps your boss' shortcoming, they have gotten away with this.

Evaluating their actions one day a week is not what you were hired for. If it were me, this is what I would tell the boss. "Unless I am their supervisor or manager I do not feel it is appropriate to report on their activities. But as a supervisor, with an appropriate title and compensation, I will get them to work on the days you are gone."

These two are not your friends. They are like misbehaving schoolchildren. Teacher is out of the room and they've gone crazy. Without authority, you might be writing yourself out of a job if you write them up. With proper authority, you could stop them from doing what they are doing.

If you are granted authority, make it clear that when the boss is out of the office, it is just another day at work.

Getting these two to work when the boss is absent is equivalent to increasing productivity by 20 percent. That kind of performance should be rewarded.

You can't write a report a supervisor would write without being a supervisor. As a supervisor, you would have protection against these two. As an equal, you have no protection.

-Tamara

A famous example of abusive friendship occurred in MI6, the British intelligence service.[10]

Kim Philby, a Soviet agent, rose to the highest levels of MI6 because he shared the same elite education, Etonian manners, and common background as others in the service. Philby compromised dozens of secrets and was responsible for the deaths of hundreds of British agents and allies.

When definitive proof of his treason was produced, Philby fled to Russia, probably aided by the laxity of another friend in the intelligence service, a Philby friend of three decades.

CHAPTER 20
CONCLUSION

Think where man's glory most begins and ends,
And say my glory was I had such friends.
—William Butler Yeats

In 1930, Joyce Hall, the founder of Hallmark Cards, proposed celebrating an annual Friendship Day. His idea never caught on, perhaps because his self-interest was too obvious. The idea languished until 1958 when Dr. Ramon Artemio Bracho sat down to dinner with friends in Paraguay and speculated how they might promote friendship.[1]

Their idea became International Friendship Day, celebrated by the United Nations on July 30. In the United States that day is bracketed on either side by National Chicken Wing Day on the 29th and National Avocado Day on the 31st.[2]

Friendship cannot be established by proclamation. It's organic. It grows or fails to grow on its own. It is palpable, yet elusive. It thrives on trust. It has rules, but the rules are unwritten.[3]

We know it when we see, and we know it when we don't see it. When it's right, it runs on autopilot; when it is wrong, it's like a rock in our shoe.

Should auld acquaintance be forgot, and never brought to mind? The answer is yes, for frenemies. For friends, the answer is no.

Back when I was in grammar school, every once in a while I would meet up with a girl my age and talk. Lisa never was around much, but she was always very sweet and nice. In 5th grade she was assigned to my class.

She was absent a lot, and one day I had the courage to ask why. She told me she was sick, and she explained she wore a wig because her medicine made her lose her hair. We left it at that. Anytime Lisa came to class—a rarity—I would hang with her on the playground.

I received much ridicule from my friends for this because they thought I was snubbing them for Lisa. My family upbringing taught me to be nice, and I felt Lisa's needs were much more important than those of others I knew.

It had been months since Lisa was in class, and one day our teacher was crying. She explained Lisa died the day before and would no longer be our classmate. She told us Lisa fought a battle with leukemia for years.

I was stunned and shocked. Lisa never spoke of her illness as if it could kill her, and I was a very innocent girl in these matters. Well, all those years I have kept Lisa in my mind and heart. When I pass milestones in my life, I reflect on Lisa and say a prayer for her.

I've had strong feelings of late to locate her mother and father. I'd like to tell them that, though they never met me, their daughter had a sweet, profound effect on my life. I have no idea what her parents' first names are and don't have money to hire a detective. I read your column and realize you are not detectives but hope you can point me in the right direction.

I pray regularly and believe something or someone is encouraging me to make this connection. I hope my connection would not hurt or upset. Lisa was such a lovely girl. Maybe her parents would be comforted that after all these years they are not the only ones who remember her.

-Cynthia

Cynthia, start with the school. You may get a lead from a former classmate, alumni group, teacher, or the parent and teacher association. Don't overlook the newspaper of record where you used to live. It probably pub-

Conclusion

lished birth and death records, including parents' names. Former neighbors may also help.

Reference librarians are invaluable. They can steer you to public government records and genealogy groups, the experts at tracking families. From among these sources, you will find someone who can help. Our lives are our relationships, and sensing a deep purpose is natural.

-Tamara

An Arab adage says: I came to the place of my birth and cried, "The friends of my youth where are they?" And echo answered, "Where are they?"

For most of us, the friends of our youth are scattered. So are friends from other times in our life. People enter our lives and leave, just as we enter their lives and leave. But our need for friendship remains.

We crave connection. That need can only be satisfied by other conscious selves—in varying degrees by animals, friends, kin, and romantic partners. It cannot be satisfied by a frenemy, a person with whom we are friendly, despite a fundamental dislike or rivalry.

Human beings have been on this planet a long time. Our genetic code has been written, rewritten, edited, copied, and misspelled. One thing that doesn't change is our need for friends.

We know who friends are. They are generous; they help in time of need; they are loyal. They treat us with dignity. We take pleasure in their company.

Our ideal friend is the equal friend, someone we are in step with, someone we walk with hand-in-hand through life.

We began this book by speaking of positive knowledge, negative knowledge, and ignorance. Positive knowledge is knowing what a friend is and how a friend acts. Negative knowledge is calling someone a friend who is a frenemy. Ignorance is being willing to learn.

We need to understand where each person fits in our life, and we need to act from that knowledge. That's a one-sentence summary of this book. As a postscript we would add, to have a friend, you must be a friend.

If we leave you with just one thought, it would be this.

Show me your friends, and I will tell you who you are.

Author Website:
WayneAndTamara.com

This book is part of Wayne & Tamara's series
Asked, Answered, and Explained.

Titles include:

Cheating in a Nutshell: What Infidelity Does to the Victim

Age Difference Relationships: When Is the Gap Insurmountable?

The Friendship Solution: Making Friends and Dropping Frenemies

NOTES

Chapter 1 – Friends and Frenemies

[1] "Definition of Frenemy." *Oxford University Press. Lexico.com*, 2021.

Chapter 2 – One Is the Loneliest Number

[1] Mendelson, Morton, and Frances Aboud. "McGill Friendship Questionnaire - Friendship Functions (MFQ-FF). Measurement Instrument Database for the Social Science."

Chapter 3 – What Is Friendship?

[1] Hruschka, Daniel *Friendship: Development, Ecology, and Evolution of a Relationship*. 45-6.

"History and Development of the HRAF Collections." Human Relations Area Files - Cultural information for education and research."

[2] Hruschka, op. cit. 48-50.

[3] Hruschka, Ibid. 2. Hruschka further defines friendships this way. "A friendship-like relationship is a social relationship in which partners provide support according to their abilities in times of need, and in which this behavior is motivated in part by positive affect between partners." 68.

[4] Heffner, Alexander. "The Neuroscience of Friendship."

[5] Holt-Lunstad, Julianne, Timothy Smith, and J. Bradley Layton. "Social Relationships and Mortality Risk: A Meta-Analytic Review."

Sohn, Emily. "More and More Research Shows Friends Are Good for Your Health."

[6] Holt-Lunstad, Julianne, Timothy Smith, Mark Baker, Tyler Harris, and David Stephenson. "Loneliness and Social Isolation as Risk Factors for Mortality."

American Psychological Association. "So Lonely I Could Die."

[7] Helliwell, John, and Haifang Huang. "Comparing the Happiness Effects of Real and On-Line Friends."

Chapter 4 – Peeling the Onion

[1] Al-Khalili, Jim (Presenter). "The Life Scientific: Robin Dunbar on Why We Have Friends."

[2] In the words of Robert Seyfarth and Dorothy Cheney, "Applying the term 'friendship' to animals is not anthropomorphic. To the contrary, many observations and experiments have shown that animals recognize the close social bonds that exist among others." Seyfarth, Robert M., and Dorothy L. Cheney. "The Evolutionary Origins of Friendship."

[3] Konnikova, Maria. "The Limits of Friendship."

[4] Dunbar, R.I.M. "Neocortex Size as a Constraint on Group Size in Primates."

[5] The 60% figure is found in: Dunbar, R. I. M. "Coevolution of Neocortical Size, Group Size and Language in Humans."

[6] From the Dunbar BBC interview. Al-Khalili, Jim (Presenter) op. cit.

Some people may be able to expand their circle of intimate friendships. See, Carlos III University of Madrid. "A Scientific Study Characterises Our Circles of Friendships." and Tamarit, Ignacio, José Cuesta, Robin Dunbar, and Angel Sánchez. "Cognitive Resource Allocation Determines the Organization of Personal Networks."

7 Konnikova, op. cit.

[8] Dunbar. "The Social Brain: Psychological Underpinnings and Implications for the Structure of Organizations."

Notes

[9] Dunbar. "Do Online Social Media Cut through the Constraints That Limit the Size of Offline Social Networks?" And *Friends: Understanding the Power of our Most Important Relationships*. 36-9, 75-6. Dunbar's book was released just as this book was going to press.

Gonçalves, Bruno, Nicola Perra, and Alessandro Vespignani. "Modeling Users' Activity on Twitter Networks: Validation of Dunbar's Number."

University of Oxford. "How Face-To-Face Still Beats Facebook."

Ohlheiser, Abby. "Even Facebook Can't Help You Have More than 150 Friends."

[10] From the Dunbar BBC interview. Al-Khalili, Jim (Presenter) op. cit.

Our friends may change, but the manner in which a particular person interacts with friends does not. Heydari, Sara, Sam Roberts, Robin Dunbar, and Jari Saramäki. "Multi-channel Social Signatures and Persistent Features of Ego Networks."

Chapter 5 – Come a Little Bit Closer

[1] Matthews, Sarah. *Friendships through the Life Course: Oral Biographies in Old Age*.

[2] Aristotle. *Nicomachean Ethics*. VIII 2-6.

[3] Almaatouq, Abdullah, Laura Radaelli, Alex Pentland, and Erez Shmueli. "Are You Your Friends' Friend? Poor Perception of Friendship Ties Limits the Ability to Promote Behavioral Change."

[4] Crew, Bec. "Only Half of Your Friends Actually like You, Science Reveals."

Murphy, Kate. "Do Your Friends Actually like You?"

[5] Williams, Lisa. "Research Check: Is It True Only Half Your Friends Actually like You?"

[6] Aron, Arthur, Elaine Aron, and Danny Smollan. "Inclusion of Other in the Self Scale and the Structure of Interpersonal Closeness."

Chapter 6 – The Doormat Syndrome

[1] Grayson, Betty, and Morris Stein. "Attracting Assault: Victims' Nonverbal Cues."

[2] Gunns, Rebekah, Lucy Johnston, and Stephen Hudson. "Victim Selection and Kinematics: A Point-Light Investigation of Vulnerability to Attack."

A nice summary of both experiments is: Stafford, Tom. "How the Way We Walk Can Increase Risk of Being Mugged."

[3] Johnston, Lucy, Stephen Hudson, Michael Richardson, Rebekah Gunns, and Megan Garner. "Changing Kinematics as a Means of Reducing Vulnerability to Physical Attack1."

[4] Namka, Lynne. *The Doormat Syndrome*. 4.

[5] Namka, ibid. 2.

[6] Seligman, Martin, and Steven Maier. "Failure to Escape Traumatic Shock."

Chapter 7 – The Answer Is No!

[1] From her poem *A Woman of a Certain Age*.

[2] Zahariades, Damon. *The Art of Saying No*. Part II.

[3] Zahariades, ibid. 6.

Chapter 8 – Your Brain Knows

[1] Nehamas, Alexander. *On Friendship*. 125-28.

[2] Parkinson, Carolyn, Adam Kleinbaum, and Thalia Wheatley. "Similar Neural Responses Predict Friendship."

[3] Parkinson, Carolyn, Adam Kleinbaum, and Thalia Wheatley. "Spontaneous Neural Encoding of Social Network Position."

Nicholas Christakis and James Fowler argue that "friends' genotypes at the single nucleotide polymorphism level tend to be positively correlated...In fact, the increase in similarity relative to strangers is at the level of fourth cousins." Most of us don't know what a fourth cousin is. It is a person with whom we share one set (out of a possible 16) of great-great-great grandparents. Christakis, Nicholas, and James Fowler. "Friendship and Natural Selection."

Chapter 9 – The Ethics of Friendship

[1] Aristotle op. cit.

Kaliarnta, Sofia. "Using Aristotle's Theory of Friendship to Classify Online Friendships: A Critical Counterview."

[2] Carlat, Daniel. "Dr. Drug Rep."

[3] Carnegie, Dale. *How to Win Friends and Influence People.*

Chapter 10 – Vouching

[1] Anderson, Digby. *Losing Friends*. 77.

Chapter 12 – The Friendship Paradox

[1] Ekman, Paul, Richard Davidson, and Wallace Friesen. "The Duchenne Smile: Emotional Expression and Brain Physiology: II."

[2] But a few people can. Gunnery, Sarah, Judith Hall, and Mollie Ruben. "The Deliberate Duchenne Smile: Individual Differences in Expressive Control."

[3] Rosenfeld, Michael, Reuben Thomas, and Sonia Hausen. "Disintermediating Your Friends: How Online Dating in the United States Displaces Other Ways of Meeting."

[4] University of Oxford, op. cit.

[5] Sherman, Lauren, Minas Michikyan, and Patricia Greenfield. "The Effects of Text, Audio, Video, and In-Person Communication on Bonding between Friends."

[6] We agree with Sofia Kaliarnta, a philosopher in The Netherlands, who said, "I propose that it is indeed necessary that greater attention should be paid to the positive sides and benefits of online friendships in a systematic way that takes into account the unique characteristics that online friendships have, and what could these kinds of friendships mean for our flourishing and well-being." Kaliarnta, op. cit.

[7] Stewart, Brian, Yuchao Zhao, Peter Mitchell, Genevieve Dewar, James Gleason, and Joel Blum. "Ostrich Eggshell Bead Strontium Isotopes Reveal Persistent Macroscale Social Networking across Late Quaternary Southern Africa."

[8] Michigan News. "Stone-Age 'Likes': Study Establishes Eggshell Beads Exchanged over 30,000 Years."

[9] Hunt, Melissa, Rachel Marx, Courtney Lipson, and Jordyn Young. "No More FOMO: Limiting Social Media Decreases Loneliness and Depression."

[10] Quotes are from: Berger, Michele. "Social Media Use Increases Depression and Loneliness."

[11] Primack, Brian, Ariel Shensa, Jaime Sidani, César Escobar-Viera, and Michael Fine. "Temporal Associations between Social Media Use and Depression."

"Increased Social Media Use Linked to Developing Depression." *NewScienceNews.com*.

Another study linking social media use with depression is: Waqas, Ali, Zamurd Khurshid, Mohsin Ali, and Habiba Khaliq. "Association between Usage of Social Media and Depression among Young Adults."

[12] Feld, Scott. "Why Your Friends Have More Friends than You Do."

[13] "How the Friendship Paradox Makes Your Friends Better than You Are." *MIT Technology Review*.

And if you are in science, your coauthors will have more coauthors, publications, and citations than you do. Eom, Young-Ho, and Hang-Hyun Jo. "Generalized Friendship Paradox in Complex Networks: The Case of Scientific Collaboration."

Notes

Chapter 13 – Ending a Friendship

[1] Epstein, Joseph. *Friendship: An Exposé.*

[2] Mollenhorst, Gerald. "Networks in Contexts: How Meeting Opportunities Affect Personal Relationships."

Mechling, Lauren. "How to End a Friendship."

[3] Lusinski, Natalia. "9 Signs It's Time to End a Friendship, according to Therapists."

[4] Schnall, Simone, Kent Harber, Jeanine Stefanucci, and Dennis Proffitt. "Social Support and the Perception of Geographical Slant."

Chapter 14 – Moving On

[1] Walker, Val. *400 Friends and No One to Call: Breaking through Isolation & Building Community.*

[2] Hall, Jeffrey. "How Many Hours Does It Take to Make a Friend?"

"How to Make Friends? Study Reveals Time It Takes." *KU News Service.*

[3] Segrin, Chris. "Indirect Effects of Social Skills on Health through Stress and Loneliness."

[4] Blue, Alexis. "Poor Social Skills May Be Harmful to Mental and Physical Health."

Chapter 15 – Jealousy

[1] What Vidal was talking about is gluckschmerz. Gluckschmerz is a German word for the feeling of unhappiness we get at the good fortune of others. A related word is schadenfreude, the feeling of pleasure we get at the misfortune of others. See, for example, Niels van de Ven: "Schadenfreude and Gluckschmerz Are Emotional Signals of (Im)Balance."

Chapter 16 – Dangerous Friends

[1] Denworth, Lydia. "The Outsize Influence of Your Middle-School Friends."

Chapter 17 – Family as Friends

[1] Madsen, Elainie, Richard Tunney, George Fieldman, Henry Plotkin, Robin Dunbar, Jean-Marie Richardson, and David McFarland. "Kinship and Altruism: A Cross-Cultural Experimental Study."

[2] Bacha-Trams, Mareike, Enrico Glerean, Robin Dunbar, Juha Lahnakoski, Elisa Ryyppö, Mikko Sams, and Iiro Jääskeläinen. "Differential Inter-Subject Correlation of Brain Activity When Kinship Is a Variable in Moral Dilemma."

[3] "Film Research Study Shows How the Brain Reacts to Difficult Moral Issues." *ScienceDaily.com*.

[4] Michener, James. *The World Is My Home: A Memoir*. 483-5.

[5] Montaigne. Michel de. *The Essays of Michel de Montaigne*. Chapter XXVII. Our paraphrase.

[6] Denworth, Lydia. *Friendship: The Evolution, Biology, and Extraordinary Power of Life's Fundamental Bond*. 149.

[7] As Daniel Hruschka says, "…humans can create kin ties with genetically unrelated partners." 80.

[8] Dunne, Michael. *Boncompagno Da Signa, 'Amicitia' and 'de Malo Senectutis et Senii'*.

Chapter 18 – Romantic Friends

[1] "Definition of Cucklord." *UrbanDictionary.com*, February 3, 2021.

[2] Perilloux, Carin, Judith Easton, and David Buss. "The Misperception of Sexual Interest."

Larsen, Rozanne. "The Misperception of Sexual Interest."

[3] Perilloux, Carin, and Robert Kurzban. "Do Men Overperceive Women's Sexual Interest?"

[4] Mongeau, Paul, Kendra Knight, Jade Williams, Jennifer Eden, and Christina Shaw. "Identifying and Explicating Variation among Friends with Benefits Relationships."

[5] Mongeau, Paul, ibid.

[6] Aron, Arthur, Edward Melinat, Elaine Aron, Robert Darrin Vallone, and Renee Bator. "The Experimental Generation of Interpersonal Closeness: A Procedure and Some Preliminary Findings."

[7] Jong, Erica. *Fear of Flying: A Novel.*

Chapter 19 – The Power of Friends

[1] "How 'Swapping Bodies' with a Friend Changes Our Sense of Self." *NeuroScienceNews.com.*

[2] Tacikowski, Pawel, Marieke Weijs, and H. Henrik Ehrsson. "Perception of Our Own Body Influences Self-Concept and Self-Incoherence Impairs Episodic Memory."

[3] Puiu, Tibi. "'Swapping Bodies' with a Friend Alters Sense of Self."

[4] Angier, Natalie. "You Share Everything with Your Bestie. Even Brain Waves."

[5] Denworth, Lydia. "The Outsize Influence..." op. cit.

[6] Chung, Seunghoo, Robert Lount, Hee Man Park, and Ernest Park. "Friends with Performance Benefits: A Meta-Analysis on the Relationship between Friendship and Group Performance."

[7] Ohio State University News. "Teams Work Better with a Little Help from Your Friends."

[8] Methot, Jessica, Jeffery Lepine, Nathan Podsakoff, and Jessica Siegel Christian. "Are Workplace Friendships a Mixed Blessing? Exploring Tradeoffs of Multiplex Relationships and Their Associations with Job Performance."

[9] Burkus, David. "Work Friends Make Us More Productive (except When They Stress Us Out)."

[10] Macintyre, Ben. *A Spy among Friends: Kim Philby and the Great Betrayal.*

Chapter 20 – Conclusion

[1] "International Friendship Day 2020: History and Significance." *Hindustan Times.*

[2] However, National Friendship Day in the United States is celebrated on the first Sunday of August. "National Friendship Day 2020: History, Significance, When Is It Celebrated in India." *Hindustan Times.*

[3] In a famous paper Michael Argyle and Monika Henderson listed six rules of friendship: standing up for a friend in their absence, sharing news of success, showing emotional support, trusting and confiding in each other, volunteering to help in a time of need, and striving to be pleasurable company. Argyle, Michael, and Monika Henderson. "The Rules of Friendship."

WORKS CITED

Al-Khalili, Jim (Presenter). "The Life Scientific: Robin Dunbar on Why We Have Friends." *BBC Radio 4*, July 23, 2019.

Almaatouq, Abdullah, Laura Radaelli, Alex Pentland, and Erez Shmueli. "Are You Your Friends' Friend? Poor Perception of Friendship Ties Limits the Ability to Promote Behavioral Change." *PLOS ONE* 11, no. 3 (March 22, 2016).

American Psychological Association. "So Lonely I Could Die." *APA.org*, August 5, 2017.

Anderson, Digby. *Losing Friends*. London: Social Affairs Unit, 2001.

Angier, Natalie. "You Share Everything with Your Bestie. Even Brain Waves." *The New York Times*, April 16, 2018.

Argyle, Michael, and Monika Henderson. "The Rules of Friendship." *Journal of Social and Personal Relationships* 1, no. 2 (June 1984).

Aristotle. *Nicomachean Ethics*. Translated by W. D. Ross. Oxford: Clarendon Press, 1908.

Aron, Arthur, Elaine Aron, and Danny Smollan. "Inclusion of Other in the Self Scale and the Structure of Interpersonal Closeness." *Journal of Personality and Social Psychology* 63, no. 4 (1992).

Aron, Arthur, Edward Melinat, Elaine Aron, Robert Darrin Vallone, and Renee Bator. "The Experimental Generation of Interpersonal Closeness: A Procedure and Some Preliminary Findings." *Personality and Social Psychology Bulletin* 23, no. 4 (April 1997).

Bacha-Trams, Mareike, Enrico Glerean, Robin Dunbar, Juha Lahnakoski, Elisa Ryyppö, Mikko Sams, and Iiro Jääskeläinen. "Differential Inter-Subject Correlation of Brain Activity When Kinship Is a Variable in Moral Dilemma." *Scientific Reports* 7, no. 1 (October 27, 2017).

Berger, Michele. "Social Media Use Increases Depression and Loneliness." *Penn Today, University of Pennsylvania*, November 9, 2018.

Blue, Alexis. "Poor Social Skills May Be Harmful to Mental and Physical Health." *University of Arizona News*, October 31, 2017.

Burkus, David. "Work Friends Make Us More Productive (except When They Stress Us Out)." *Harvard Business Review - HBR.org*, May 26, 2017.

Carlat, Daniel. "Dr. Drug Rep." *The New York Times*, November 25, 2007.

Carlos III University of Madrid. "A Scientific Study Characterises Our Circles of Friendships." *Phy.org*, July 23, 2018.

Christakis, Nicholas, and James Fowler. "Friendship and Natural Selection." *Proceedings of the National Academy of Sciences* 111, Supplement 3 (July 22, 2014).

Chung, Seunghoo, Robert Lount, Hee Man Park, and Ernest Park. "Friends with Performance Benefits: A Meta-Analysis on the Relationship between Friendship and Group Performance." *Personality and Social Psychology Bulletin* 44, no. 1 (October 10, 2017).

Crew, Bec. "Only Half of Your Friends Actually like You, Science Reveals." *ScienceDirect.com*, May 1, 2018.

"Definition of Cucklord." *UrbanDictionary.com*, February 3, 2021.

"Definition of Frenemy." *Oxford University Press. Lexico.com*, March 4, 2021.

Denworth, Lydia. *Friendship: The Evolution, Biology, and Extraordinary Power of Life's Fundamental Bond*. New York: W.W. Norton, 2020.

———. "The Outsize Influence of Your Middle-School Friends." *TheAlantic.com*, January 28, 2020.

Dunbar, R. I. M. "Coevolution of Neocortical Size, Group Size and Language in Humans." *Behavioral and Brain Sciences* 16, no. 4 (December 1993).

———. "Do Online Social Media Cut through the Constraints That Limit the Size of Offline Social Networks?" *Royal Society Open Science* 3, no. 1 (January 2016).

———. "The Social Brain: Psychological Underpinnings and Implications for the Structure of Organizations." *Current Directions in Psychological Science* 23, no. 2 (April 2014).

———. "Neocortex Size as a Constraint on Group Size in Primates." *Journal of Human Evolution* 22, no. 6 (June 1992).

Dunne, Michael. *Boncompagno Da Signa, 'Amicitia' and 'de Malo Senectutis et Senii'*. Leuven: Peeters, 2012.

Ekman, Paul, Richard Davidson, and Wallace Friesen. "The Duchenne Smile: Emotional Expression and Brain Physiology: II." *Journal of Personality and Social Psychology* 58, no. 2 (1990).

Eom, Young-Ho, and Hang-Hyun Jo. "Generalized Friendship Paradox in Complex Networks: The Case of Scientific Collaboration." *Scientific Reports* 4, no. 1 (April 8, 2014).

Epstein, Joseph. *Friendship: An Exposé*. Boston: Houghton Mifflin, 2006.

Feld, Scott. "Why Your Friends Have More Friends than You Do." *American Journal of Sociology* 96, no. 6 (May 1991).

"Film Research Study Shows How the Brain Reacts to Difficult Moral Issues." *ScienceDaily.com*, October 27, 2017.

Gonçalves, Bruno, Nicola Perra, and Alessandro Vespignani. "Modeling Users' Activity on Twitter Networks: Validation of Dunbar's Number." Edited by Matjaz Perc. *PLoS ONE* 6, no. 8 (August 3, 2011).

Grayson, Betty, and Morris Stein. "Attracting Assault: Victims' Nonverbal Cues." *Journal of Communication* 31, no. 1 (March 1, 1981).

Gunnery, Sarah, Judith Hall, and Mollie Ruben. "The Deliberate Duchenne Smile: Individual Differences in Expressive Control." *Journal of Nonverbal Behavior* 37, no. 1 (October 13, 2012).

Gunns, Rebekah, Lucy Johnston, and Stephen Hudson. "Victim Selection and Kinematics: A Point-Light Investigation of Vulnerability to Attack." *Journal of Nonverbal Behavior* 26, no. 3 (September 2002).

Hall, Jeffrey. "How Many Hours Does It Take to Make a Friend?" *Journal of Social and Personal Relationships* 36, no. 4 (March 15, 2018).

Heffner, Alexander. "The Neuroscience of Friendship." *The American Prospect*, February 9, 2020.

Helliwell, John, and Haifang Huang. "Comparing the Happiness Effects of Real and On-Line Friends." Edited by Cédric Sueur. *PLOS ONE* 8, no. 9 (September 3, 2013).

Heydari, Sara, Sam Roberts, Robin Dunbar, and Jari Saramäki. "Multichannel Social Signatures and Persistent Features of Ego Networks." *Applied Network Science* 3, no. 1 (May 29, 2018).

"History and Development of the HRAF Collections." Human Relations Area Files - Cultural information for education and research, November 14, 2013. https://hraf.yale.edu/about/history-and-development/.

Holt-Lunstad, Julianne, Timothy Smith, Mark Baker, Tyler Harris, and David Stephenson. "Loneliness and Social Isolation as Risk Factors for Mortality." *Perspectives on Psychological Science* 10, no. 2 (March 2015).

Holt-Lunstad, Julianne, Timothy Smith, and J. Bradley Layton. "Social Relationships and Mortality Risk: A Meta-Analytic Review." *PLOS Medicine* 7, no. 7 (July 27, 2010).

"How 'Swapping Bodies' with a Friend Changes Our Sense of Self." *NeuroScienceNews.com*, August 26, 2020.

"How the Friendship Paradox Makes Your Friends Better than You Are." *MIT Technology Review*, January 14, 2014.

Works Cited

"How to Make Friends? Study Reveals Time It Takes." *KU News Service*, March 28, 2018.

Hruschka, Daniel. *Friendship: Development, Ecology, and Evolution of a Relationship.* Berkeley, California: University Of California Press, 2010.

Hunt, Melissa, Rachel Marx, Courtney Lipson, and Jordyn Young. "No More FOMO: Limiting Social Media Decreases Loneliness and Depression." *Journal of Social and Clinical Psychology* 37, no. 10 (December 2018).

"Increased Social Media Use Linked to Developing Depression." *NewScienceNews.com*, December 12, 2020.

"International Friendship Day 2020: History and Significance." *Hindustan Times*, July 25, 2020.

Johnston, Lucy, Stephen Hudson, Michael Richardson, Rebekah Gunns, and Megan Garner. "Changing Kinematics as a Means of Reducing Vulnerability to Physical Attack1." *Journal of Applied Social Psychology* 34, no. 3 (March 2004).

Jong, Erica. *Fear of Flying: A Novel.* Berkley, reprint edition. New York: Vintage Books, 2003.

Kaliarnta, Sofia. "Using Aristotle's Theory of Friendship to Classify Online Friendships: A Critical Counterview." *Ethics and Information Technology* 18, no. 2 (January 22, 2016).

Konnikova, Maria. "The Limits of Friendship." *The New Yorker*, October 7, 2014.

Larsen, Rozanne. "The Misperception of Sexual Interest." *Journalist's Resource*, April 20, 2012.

Lusinski, Natalia. "9 Signs It's Time to End a Friendship, according to Therapists." *Business Insider*, December 9, 2018.

Macintyre, Ben. *A Spy among Friends: Kim Philby and the Great Betrayal.* New York: Crown, 2014.

Madsen, Elainie, Richard Tunney, George Fieldman, Henry Plotkin, Robin Dunbar, Jean-Marie Richardson, and David McFarland. "Kinship and Altruism: A Cross-Cultural Experimental Study." *British Journal of Psychology* 98, no. 2 (May 2007).

Matthews, Sarah. *Friendships through the Life Course: Oral Biographies in Old Age*. Beverly Hills: Sage Publications, 1986.

Mechling, Lauren. "How to End a Friendship." *The New York Times*, June 14, 2019.

Mendelson, Morton, and Frances Aboud. "McGill Friendship Questionnaire - Friendship Functions (MFQ-FF). Measurement Instrument Database for the Social Science." 2014.

Methot, Jessica, Jeffery Lepine, Nathan Podsakoff, and Jessica Siegel Christian. "Are Workplace Friendships a Mixed Blessing? Exploring Tradeoffs of Multiplex Relationships and Their Associations with Job Performance." *Personnel Psychology* 69, no. 2 (November 5, 2015).

Michener, James. *The World Is My Home: A Memoir*. New York: Random House, 1992.

Michigan News. "Stone-Age 'Likes': Study Establishes Eggshell Beads Exchanged over 30,000 Years." *University of Michigan*, March 9, 2020.

Mollenhorst, Gerald. "Networks in Contexts: How Meeting Opportunities Affect Personal Relationships." *Utrecht University Repository (Dissertation)*, 2009.

Mongeau, Paul, Kendra Knight, Jade Williams, Jennifer Eden, and Christina Shaw. "Identifying and Explicating Variation among Friends with Benefits Relationships." *Journal of Sex Research* 50, no. 1 (January 2013).

Montaigne. *The Essays of Michel de Montaigne*. Edited by William Carew Hazlitt. Translated by Charles Cotton. Project Gutenberg, 1877.

Murphy, Kate. "Do Your Friends Actually like You?" *The New York Times*, August 6, 2016.

Namka, Lynne. *The Doormat Syndrome*. Iuniverse.com (reprint), 2000.

Works Cited

"National Friendship Day 2020: History, Significance, When Is It Celebrated in India." *Hindustan Times*, August 1, 2020.

Nehamas, Alexander. *On Friendship*. New York: Basic Books, 2016.

Ohio State University News. "Teams Work Better with a Little Help from Your Friends." October 23, 2017.

Ohlheiser, Abby. "Even Facebook Can't Help You Have More than 150 Friends." *Washington Post*, January 20, 2016.

Parkinson, Carolyn, Adam Kleinbaum, and Thalia Wheatley. "Similar Neural Responses Predict Friendship." *Nature Communications* 9, no. 1 (January 30, 2018).

———. "Spontaneous Neural Encoding of Social Network Position." *Nature Human Behaviour* 1, no. 5 (April 18, 2017).

Perilloux, Carin, Judith Easton, and David Buss. "The Misperception of Sexual Interest." *Psychological Science* 23, no. 2 (January 18, 2012).

Perilloux, Carin, and Robert Kurzban. "Do Men Overperceive Women's Sexual Interest?" *Psychological Science* 26, no. 1 (November 20, 2014).

Primack, Brian, Ariel Shensa, Jaime Sidani, César Escobar-Viera, and Michael Fine. "Temporal Associations between Social Media Use and Depression." *American Journal of Preventive Medicine*, December 2020.

Puiu, Tibi. "'Swapping Bodies' with a Friend Alters Sense of Self." ZMEScience.com, August 26, 2020.

Rosenfeld, Michael, Reuben Thomas, and Sonia Hausen. "Disintermediating Your Friends: How Online Dating in the United States Displaces Other Ways of Meeting." *Proceedings of the National Academy of Sciences* 116, no. 36 (August 20, 2019).

Schnall, Simone, Kent Harber, Jeanine Stefanucci, and Dennis Proffitt. "Social Support and the Perception of Geographical Slant." *Journal of Experimental Social Psychology* 44, no. 5 (September 2008).

Segrin, Chris. "Indirect Effects of Social Skills on Health through Stress and Loneliness." *Health Communication* 34, no. 1 (October 20, 2017).

Seligman, Martin, and Steven Maier. "Failure to Escape Traumatic Shock." *Journal of Experimental Psychology* 74, no. 1 (1967).

Seyfarth, Robert, and Dorothy Cheney. "The Evolutionary Origins of Friendship." *Annual Review of Psychology* 63, no. 1 (January 10, 2012).

Sherman, Lauren, Minas Michikyan, and Patricia Greenfield. "The Effects of Text, Audio, Video, and In-Person Communication on Bonding between Friends." *Cyberpsychology: Journal of Psychosocial Research on Cyberspace* 7, no. 2 (2013).

Sohn, Emily. "More and More Research Shows Friends Are Good for Your Health." *Washington Post*, May 26, 2016.

Stafford, Tom. "How the Way We Walk Can Increase Risk of Being Mugged." *BBC.com*, November 4, 2013.

Stewart, Brian, Yuchao Zhao, Peter Mitchell, Genevieve Dewar, James Gleason, and Joel Blum. "Ostrich Eggshell Bead Strontium Isotopes Reveal Persistent Macroscale Social Networking across Late Quaternary Southern Africa." *Proceedings of the National Academy of Sciences* 117, no. 12 (March 9, 2020).

Tacikowski, Pawel, Marieke Weijs, and H. Henrik Ehrsson. "Perception of Our Own Body Influences Self-Concept and Self-Incoherence Impairs Episodic Memory." *IScience* 23, no. 9 (September 2020).

Tamarit, Ignacio, José Cuesta, Robin Dunbar, and Angel Sánchez. "Cognitive Resource Allocation Determines the Organization of Personal Networks." *Proceedings of the National Academy of Sciences* 115, no. 33 (July 26, 2018).

University of Oxford. "How Face-To-Face Still Beats Facebook." (*Www.ox.ac.uk/News/*), January 20, 2016.

Ven, Niels van de. "Schadenfreude and Gluckschmerz Are Emotional Signals of (Im)Balance." *Emotion Review* 10, no. 4 (August 9, 2018).

Walker, Val. *400 Friends and No One to Call: Breaking through Isolation & Building Community*. Las Vegas: Central Recovery Press, 2020.

Waqas, Ali, Zamurd Khurshid, Mohsin Ali, and Habiba Khaliq. "Association between Usage of Social Media and Depression among Young Adults." *Journal of Management Info* 5, no. 4 (December 31, 2018).

Williams, Lisa "Research Check: Is It True Only Half Your Friends Actually like You?" *The Conversation*. August 17, 2016.

"Your Brain Reveals Who Your Friends Are." *NeuroScienceNews.com*, January 30, 2018.

Zahariades, Damon. *The Art of Saying No*. ArtOfProductivity.com, 2017.

www.ingramcontent.com/pod-product-compliance
Lightning Source LLC
Chambersburg PA
CBHW060104230426
43661CB00033B/1417/J